In this very moving account of a yo[...] courageously allows us a large wind[...] despair, self-pity and anger. Clingin[...] she discovers that he has inner surg [...] attitudes. After going through three years of intense pain, Janine emerges with God having drawn her more deeply to himself and revealed to her a true identity along with the gifts he wants to use. There is much to learn from this story about good pastoral guidance. When I had reached the last page I could only exclaim, 'Glory to God!'
Bishop Graham Dow

Janine shares simply and honestly her personal feelings of lost identity brought about by the death of her husband. She faces the anger, self-reliance, low self-esteem and brokenness she discovers buried in the depths of her being – and shares her choice to accept these unpalatable truths and move on. Through the pain, she transitions from self-pity to a place where she recognizes grief itself as a gift of God enabling her to love more deeply.
Jacqui Frost, textile artist and fellow-traveller on the path of grief

Having both suffered the heartache of the death of our previous partners while we were in our thirties, we can thoroughly recommend Janine Fair's book. She tells the story of her journey honestly – through shock, pain, grief and despair to hope for the future and a new and fulfilled life.
Joy and Bob Jones, Care for the Family's 'A Different Journey' (supporting those widowed at a young age)

Bereavement is a path that no-one can walk for you, but the experience of those who have already walked through it can be a soothing help. This is the case in *Surprised by Grief*, a moving personal story where the author blends her very personal feelings with a lot of practical and biblical wisdom.

I warmly recommend this excellent book for all those who want to learn how to transform grief into a gift from God.
Dr. Pablo Martinez, Psychiatrist, and co-author of Tracing the Rainbow: Walking Through Loss and Bereavement

A moving book that powerfully expresses the reality of loss. Its particular strength lies in the author's willingness to share her deepest feelings of shame, anger, bitterness and self-pity. She exposes the full extent of her desolation as well as the real challenges of her relationship with God.

However, it is ultimately a story of hope as she finally finds goodness in her desolation and God's grace in her life. This book will help anyone in the same situation and those of us who want to offer support to the bereaved.
Julia Ogilvy, Chair of ProjectScotland and the author of Turning Points

What a great book! I was sad, happy, surprised – quite an emotional Saturday night.

The thrust of the writing is about Janine's own feelings, thoughts and attitudes following the death of her husband. *Surprised by Grief* is a very apt title and reflects the surprise I felt at some of the discoveries that Janine shares from her journey into and through grief. As I read, I was sucked into the loss and desperation that Janine felt: I admired her brutal honesty about herself and her journey, and I was fascinated by the career change.

But for me there was a truly 'wow' moment which made me want to read and reread her revelation, that God in his amazing love had given her pain and trauma, unwrapped, undecorated, with no pretty tag or ribbons, but as wonderful gifts for which she can now give thanks. I was greatly inspired and my heart rose in praise!
Greta Randle, Chief Executive, Association of Christian Counsellors and author of Forgiving the Impossible? From Abuse to Freedom and Hope

For anyone bereaved, this book brings life and hope. Clergy wife Janine Fair describes with heart-wrenching honesty the shock of the sudden death of her husband and the arduous and long journey of her ensuing grief, showing that, despite the devastation of grief, beauty and happiness really can emerge.

As a minister myself recently widowed, I appeal to all potentially involved in bereavement ministry to hear the pain of these words and respond with long-term understanding and love. And to those who share this deep and dark tunnel, may Janine's story bring the seeds of healing you deserve.
Revd Canon Yvonne Richmond, Birmingham Cathedral

Honest, absorbing and deeply moving, Janine's account of her own path of pain and journey of faith gives great insight for those travelling this road themselves or seeking to help others find hope and courage amidst the turmoil of grief.
Alison Risbridger, Ministry Assistant at Above Bar Church, Southampton

This is a diary of terrible pain and strong faith, not competing with each other, neither obliterating the other. It is a powerful read, sometimes almost unbearably so. It is also a deeply hopeful one: this book declares by its message and by its very existence that it is possible to experience God's grace and wisdom even through a time of terrible loss and inner turbulence. Janine Fair writes with intimate candour about her unfinished journey from a place of hope and trust.
Peter Selby, Bishop of Worcester 1997–2007

From her account of the sudden and shocking death of her husband, to her subsequent struggles to rebuild her life, Janine Fair writes with great honesty about her journey through grief and her gradual acceptance of the future God has for her.
Jackie Stead, Editor of Woman Alive

Surprised by Grief

Janine Fair

Surprised by Grief

A journey into hope

ivp

INTER-VARSITY PRESS
Norton Street, Nottingham NG7 3HR, England
Email: ivp@ivpbooks.com
Website: www.ivpbooks.com

British Library Cataloguing in Publication Data
A catalogue record for this book is available from the British Library.

ISBN: 978–1–84474–472–5

Set in 10.5/14pt Chaparral
Typeset in Great Britain by CRB Associates, Potterhanworth, Lincolnshire
Printed in Great Britain by Ashford Colour Press Ltd, Gosport, Hampshire

Inter-Varsity Press publishes Christian books that are true to the Bible and
that communicate the gospel, develop discipleship and strengthen the
church for its mission in the world.

Inter-Varsity Press is closely linked with the Universities and Colleges
Christian Fellowship, a student movement connecting Christian Unions
in universities and colleges throughout Great Britain, and a member
movement of the International Fellowship of Evangelical Students.
Website: www.uccf.org.uk

Contents

Acknowledgments

There are so many people to whom I wish to express my thanks, all of whom have played their part in the writing of *Surprised by Grief*.

First, I want to say a big thank you to my editor, for believing in the value of this book, and to my coach, for her enthusiasm and encouragement as I first began to write.

Secondly, I need to express my heartfelt gratitude to my loyal family and friends, for standing by me through the worst ravages of my grief, and for giving me their unending support, even as I found myself reliving my pain in agonizing detail as I wrote. I am more grateful than you will ever understand.

And thirdly, I must thank my two amazing children, for living with me through all my ups and downs, and for loving me and forgiving me, even when my grief was so overwhelming that I was unable to help them with theirs. Thank you for being yourselves. I love you both enormously.

But my greatest thank you has to go to God, for all that he has done for me. There are not words enough to express the gratitude I feel. That he could use even the devastation of my grief to draw me closer to his side is a marvellous mystery that I can never hope fully to understand.

Dedication

To my Heavenly Father and my Lord, without whom this whole journey would have been impossible.

Introduction

Losing a partner to death at a young age is a devastating experience. I know. I've been there. My husband, Richard, died suddenly in his sleep in June 2004, leaving me to cope alone with two young children.[1] It felt as if my world had imploded as my biggest nightmare became reality literally overnight. The familiar landmarks of my life became taunts, reminding me of my loss. My path had to be renegotiated almost from scratch, and the scenery felt like a barren wilderness. My sense of identity was completely shaken, my direction in life radically altered, and I felt utterly lost.

I clung to the 'normalities' of life: looking after the children, and running the home as best I could. While superficially I looked as if I was coping, often I was weeping inside. I was weeping for the dreams I had lost and the hopes I would never see materialize. My desolate loneliness felt overwhelming at times, and I longed to find an easier route.

Navigating my way through grief felt utterly terrifying, so I read all the books I could find, hoping for some handle

---

[1] I have deliberately chosen not to name my children in this book, both in order to protect them as they grow up, and because this book is about my journey through grief and not theirs.

on to which I could cling. And yet, even as I sought to hold on to what others had learnt, I knew that my journey would be unique, and that I would have to make my own route through my pain. I clung to God and his promises as lifelines, certain that without him I would fall. And I determined as best I could to press on to find a future filled with hope.

The path through my grief has, however, been much more gruelling than I first thought it would be. It has sapped me of my energy and drained me of my joy. I have needed huge quantities of grit, determination and courage to keep pressing on. At times the frustration has been great indeed, as I have impatiently attempted to leave the past behind, and my endurance has been sorely tested as the future has been so slow to appear.

But through it all God has been my constant companion and guide. It was he who gave me the strength and grace to continue, and my journey through grief is a testimony to the way that his love has drawn me on.

My journey has been full of learning and growth, as well as a vast amount of pain, and it has taken me many tear-filled nights (and tissues!) to get to the point where I can now look back with gratitude for all that God has done. And as he has enabled that gratitude to rise within, I have been able to see the priceless gifts that he has strewn along my way: gifts that have been shot through with both joy and pain. It seems that through all the devastation I have experienced, God has been wooing me to himself. He has put up with my petty pride and my self-pitying despair, persistently holding out his arms of love to me, and meeting what willingness and courage I did possess with an abundance of his grace.

As he has met me within the crucible of my pain, I have begun to understand something of the toughness and resilience of his love. That the Creator of the universe could have such unconditional love for me continues to bowl me over day after day.

My hope is that, by sharing something of my journey through grief in the pages of this book, you too will encounter the vastness and richness of God's love, as demonstrated by Jesus' death on the cross.

Janine Fair
November 2009

1 Journey into the unknown

It was the middle of June 2004. Rolling over in bed in the half-light, I was frustrated to have been awoken early yet again from my sleep. It was just after 4am. Unable to work out the reason for my premature awakening, I got up to listen carefully for some sound from the children. Suddenly I became aware of a strange rasping noise coming from the far side of the bed. I peered at Richard through the semi-darkness, expecting to see him sleeping soundly and thus allay my fears. But the oddness of the sound unnerved me, and I was unable to settle. I looked again, and as I did so, the noises changed to a gurgle. Gradually I was becoming more and more awake. My brain wouldn't compute correctly, and as I listened, the breaths became less frequent and the noises died away. I was unable to grasp the significance of what I was hearing. Richard's limbs were twitching now and a wet patch was appearing on the bed where he lay. What was going on? My mind struggled to take it all on board.

The only thing I could think of was that Richard was having an epileptic fit. Hastily I rolled him over into the recovery position, feeling clumsy and foolish, and wondering how I would explain it all to him when he awoke. My brain felt sluggish and sleepy, and my thoughts were less than coherent. I was struggling to know how to react. Slowly it began to dawn on me that I needed to ring for help. I hurriedly scrambled to the phone and dialled 999.

The operator's questions cut through the remnants of my sleepiness at once. Was he still breathing? I didn't know. I knelt down close to his face, ashamed I had not thought to check. Desperately I looked for some sign that his chest was rising and felt for some wisp of breath on my cheek. Surely this couldn't be happening to me, to him, right now? There must be some mistake. I lingered as long as I dared, hoping that my fears were unfounded and it was simply my imagination running rife. But the breath never came, and Richard's body lay lifeless and still. An icy finger began to claw at my mind.

The voice of the operator broke into my awareness again. Was there a pulse? My trembling fingers felt in the groove where the pulse should be, but it was no use. The only pulse was mine as my heart hammered away wildly in my chest. I was fully awake now, and a great cry was rising up inside of me, a cry that wanted to deny the reality of what I was witnessing, a cry of intense shock and pain. A shiver went through my body as an icy hand took hold of my heart. Slowly my mind began to take in the gravity of the situation before me. Richard was on his way out. What I had heard had been a death rattle, something I only dimly remembered from my previous medical training.

The operator was there again, insisting I take notice, and issuing instructions. By now I knew that any medical objectivity I might have hoped for had vanished, and I was swamped by the subjectivity of my responses. I was in this as someone's lover, as Richard's wife, not as a medic on a hospital ward. Directions were coming thick and fast, and I was urged to try to get him to the floor. I panicked, seeing only a thin sliver of floor on his side of the bed, and I realized I would have to get him over to the opposite edge. I heaved with all my might, but the dead weight of Richard's body quickly defeated me, and I panicked again. Everything was depending on me now, and I was filled with fear. I didn't want to let Richard down, and yet I desperately wished to escape.

Instructions for resuscitation started coming thick and fast. There was no time to process my emotions right now; I had to listen and obey. Gratefully I accepted each command as it was uttered, and tried to keep my mind from running ahead.

Anxiously I wrenched Richard's head back, desperately trying to open his airway, and I blew into his dry, still lips. The lack of response and the coldness of his lips sent a shiver down my spine; a large lump began to form in my throat. I had to concentrate on staying in the moment and begin to give him breaths even though it all felt so wrong. But the breaths I gave made no difference, and my heart began to race; I knew I would need to do more. Kneeling over his body I pressed down on his sternum, and as I did so I heard a crack. The noise frightened me, and added to my growing sense of alarm and ineptitude. I had just broken his rib. I altered my position and resumed action. Now began a gruelling round of breaths followed by chest compressions with the operator talking me through each stage, me bouncing on the bed as I made each move, desperately longing for some indication that my efforts were not in vain. It seemed so unreal, as if I was stuck in a very bad dream. I had never liked emergency medicine, and now here I was doing it in my own home on the one I loved most in the world. How could this be happening? It couldn't be true. Not here. Not now. Not with him.

The physical effort of the resuscitation attempt was immense. My wrists were aching, and I was out of breath. I could not continue this way for long, especially while my mind was racing so much and trying to work it all out. Again

I made a conscious decision to shelve my burning questions, and poured everything I could into the task before me. I had to go on. I could not stop to think about the incongruity of it all, and how wrong it all felt. And still the only response I got was Richard's pallid, lifeless form stretched out in front of me, and the repeated words of the operator, urging me on.

In desperation I looked out of the window, searching the greyness for some sign of the ambulance, while trying to give my utmost to the resuscitation attempt. I was nearing the limits of my exhaustion, uncertain how much longer I could go on.

At last the blue light came into view, and I flung open the window, eager to show them where I was. My relief at no longer being alone was palpable as I dashed down the stairs and threw open the door. I began garbling as soon as the paramedics were within earshot, blurting out anything I could think of that might help them in their job.

But my feelings of relief were quickly replaced by an increasing sense of doom as they swiftly took control. Their faces betrayed what they were thinking, and their expressions were grim. I felt raw and humiliated, as if I was somehow to blame and my utter incompetence as a wife and a doctor had been brutally exposed. I knew that the resuscitation attempt had not been perfect, and I wished I had not compounded Richard's fragile state by breaking his rib. How could I ever hold up my head again or look myself in the eye? Quickly I pushed my self-admonishments to one side, and fought hard to stay in touch with the present moment.

The paramedics made it look so easy as they swiftly moved Richard's body to the floor. I began to rebuke myself again. If only I had managed to do that, then my resuscitation attempt would not have been so fruitless. I watched helplessly as they slashed his pyjamas open and attached pads and leads, not wanting to accept what was going on before my eyes. Within seconds, a faint thin line had traced itself across the defibrillator screen. It couldn't be! I knew that signal, but surely there was some mistake? I watched as Richard's body arched with the increasing shocks they were giving him, shocks that left me reeling inside. I had seen enough. I ran to the bathroom and threw on some clothes as I fought back the tears.

My mind was racing. The children. What about the children? Please, Jesus, let them sleep through all this noise. The paramedics were now hauling Richard's pale, limp body on to a chair, and telling me to ring a friend. Hastily I grabbed my diary and found a number to call. There was no time to lose. 'It's Richard. He's not breathing well. I have to go with him to the hospital,' was all I could think to say.

It was enough, and I put the phone down. My mind was doing overtime now. I needed to pack a bag. I shoved in my diary, purse and phone, and Richard's medication. In utter denial, I picked up spare clothes and underwear for Richard for when he came around. I desperately wanted to believe that he would need them, even though in my heart I knew that it would not be so. I followed behind as they hastily bumped him down the stairs, wincing as his flaccid body jolted with every move.

A neighbour, alerted by the commotion, came to the door and offered to stay in the house while I was gone. Gratefully I accepted as I took a seat in the back of the ambulance. I felt numb, shaking inside and out, too scared to take in the impact of what I had just observed.

I clung to the side of the ambulance as the driver flung us around corners at top speed. The inside of the ambulance seemed so clinical and cold, and Richard's body on the other side of the vehicle seemed so far away. I offered to help as the paramedic struggled to continue the resuscitation attempt, clutching at the chance to do something useful again. But the mask would not seal properly around Richard's drooping mouth, and the oxygen kept leaking out. I just had to persevere, despite the tears that were longing to be allowed to trickle down my face.

On arrival at the hospital, the ambulance doors were flung open and I instinctively moved aside, anxious not to get in the way. Time was running out. I felt weak and powerless as Richard's body disappeared from sight. I was shivering now, the coolness of the morning air compounding the icy chill I felt inside. I made my way indoors. New drugs were being given to Richard and a fresh round of shocks. I found it hard to keep up with everything that was going on. But the monitors showed no response, and any residual hope began to drain away. It was futile now. Richard's brain and heart had been starved of oxygen for too long.

There was an embarrassed silence as the team paused to take stock. Suddenly I became conscious that all eyes were on me, as if I was an unwanted intruder. I felt an outsider here, not one of the team, and I found myself being gently steered away. In desperation I spoke up. I had come this far with him, and was not prepared to abandon him now. I declared my medical credentials and begged to be allowed to remain. Reluctantly they agreed as round two of the resuscitation attempt began.

But the mutterings from the team continued and I could see that their enthusiasm had slackened. It felt as if they were going through the motions purely for my sake, and their faces belied their lack of hope. I scanned the screens for one last time. They were right. No flicker from his heart at any point. To go on was a waste of time. The words came, half strangled, out of my lips, 'It's okay, you can stop. I know he's gone.' I needed to hear the words for myself as much as they did. Relieved, the team stood back, and a sheet was drawn across Richard's face.

A tidal wave of emotions hit me all at once. I felt so silly standing there looking at where Richard's face had been, and

I felt insulted that they had hidden him from view. It was my husband they were dealing with, and I was not yet ready to let him go. I didn't want to take my eyes off him just yet, he who was the centre of my world and whose body I had come to know so well. I wanted to rush over to him, to hold him in my arms, and to hug him one last time. I didn't want things to end on this note, with Richard's final moments being spent on a cold, clinical hospital trolley surrounded by medical equipment and personnel. I didn't want this to be the end. If only there had been time to say 'I love you' one last time, and to hold his hand tenderly as he had quietly slipped away. Instead Richard had been stripped half naked and surrounded by a well-meaning but unknown medical team who had riddled his body with needles and drugs.

Once again I found myself being steered gently out of the room as the tidying up began. I did not know what they would do to him now, but it felt so hard. It was my husband they were cleaning up, and I wanted to be present. I wanted to make sure they treated him with respect as the tubes and needles were being removed, and to ensure that he was given all the dignity that he deserved. I felt cheated of the chance to be part of this last act of service.

Instead I was led away to a quiet side room to wait on my own. The medical team had barely been able to meet my eyes as one by one they had left the resuscitation room. They seemed more stunned than me, shaking their heads in disbelief that one who was so young could die so suddenly in this way.

Sitting in that side room all alone was agony itself. The room was tastefully furnished and yet there was no comfort in there for me. I glanced at the patterned wallpaper and remembered the times when I as a doctor had sat in rooms such as this, talking with relatives who had been bereaved. It felt too awful to accept that it was now my turn. I looked at the telephone I had been encouraged to use, and wondered whom I should ring. The one I most wanted to speak to was now dead, and I felt too raw to speak to anyone else. Besides it was still very early; it seemed pointless to disturb people's sleep.

My mind wandered back to my friend waiting at home, and I realized that in all the commotion I hadn't even managed to see her arrive before the ambulance had left. She would want to know what was happening, and so I shakily picked up the telephone. In a daze I rang and gave her the news. It felt too much for anyone to take in. My voice sounded distant and strained as I briefly ran through what had happened, and reassured her I would soon be home.

My mind felt numb. The icy coldness that had started to creep around my mind and heart earlier had now spread to encircle my whole body, and I felt chilled to the core. It was as if a thick blanket of snow had come to settle inside of me, cutting me off from the warmth outside. Nothing seemed very real right now, except that feeling of coldness penetrating all through my being, and I clutched instinctively at my bag, as if something tangible would help me regain control. I felt lost and confused, and utterly stunned.

After a while a nurse came to fetch me. I followed as we made our way to a back room, not knowing what to say. I knew that they would have done their best to make Richard look peaceful and at rest, but could think no further than that. He had been clothed in a sterile white hospital gown, and the sight of him, so silent and devoid of colour, made me want to retch and scream. This couldn't be real. This was not my Richard, the one I had embraced last night and the one I loved so much. There had to be some mistake. I had to get closer, to touch him and to feel his skin, to let the reality sink in.

It was obvious to me that he was not there. What I was looking at was merely his shell. The flimsy washed-out gown accentuated the cold whiteness of his skin. Even the pale curtains seemed to mock me as they flapped nonchalantly in the cool morning breeze.

In the stillness of this room, away from all the noise and bustle, I was supposed to say my goodbyes. But how could I say goodbye to one who only hours before had been so alive and well? I stood there, letting the tears roll down my face as I gently ran my fingers through his hair. There were no words to say except 'I love you', words I wished I had been able to say before it was too late. I had been so caught up in the urgency of the resuscitation attempt that the moment had passed without me even realizing it. This sudden stillness was a stark contrast to the frenetic activity of such a short time before.

A prayer found its way to my lips as I implored God to do the impossible and bring Richard back to life. And yet even as I said it I knew I could not ask for that now. To do so would be to call Richard back from the place he had longed to go to for so long. How could I do that to him?

The silence of the ward began to unnerve me, and I needed to get out. I wanted to run from this place and discover it had all been a bad dream. I felt as if we were an embarrassment to the medical establishment because Richard had not come round, and the team's sense of failure was only matched by mine. I found myself longing to be at home, to be with those who knew and loved me, rather than the nameless hospital staff whom I would never see again.

A different nurse came to collect me and lead me away, leaving me to sit alone and forlorn on the cold plastic seats in the porch to wait for a taxi to take me home. In my hand was a thin plastic bag containing the remnants of Richard's torn pyjamas, all I had left to insulate me against the coldness of the pain. There was no activity now, just the drone of the hospital lights, and no-one else in sight.

Eventually the taxi arrived. I took my seat cautiously and wished I could be instantly transported home. The taxi driver seemed to want to know all about me and why I was there at such an early hour alone. I did my best to explain, desperately hoping that the conversation would cease so I could collect my thoughts. But it seemed that he needed to talk to let his feelings out, and I listened in disbelief as he spoke about reincarnation and how it made everything all right. I tried to push down the growing anger and revulsion inside, frustrated that my need for peace had been totally ignored, and began to count the minutes until I would be safely home. The children would be waking soon, and I wanted the chance to think through how I would tell them the shocking news. I let the driver's words wash over me as he continued.

My friend was waiting to embrace me as I finally made my way indoors. Thankfully the children were as yet oblivious, and we had a few moments together to help me steady myself. I felt utterly shattered and totally drained, yet I knew the day had barely begun. My first hurdle would be to break the news to the children, and I was not looking forward to that. They were still so young and I wasn't sure what reaction I would get. Would they be able to take it in, or would it all be too much? But I knew I needed to tell them the truth. Daddy was gone. I could not hide it from them. I prayed that they would be able to take in what I had to say.

My mind flew back to an incident the week before when our three-year-old had discovered a dead mouse outside. I had spent some time talking with the children then about death and how our physical bodies are left behind. At the time I had wondered at the strangeness of the incident, worrying that I had said too much and overburdened them at such a young age. Now, just a few days later, it seemed as if it had been a gift, offering me an easy way in to break the news. My children were about to experience the full shocking reality of death in their own tiny lives.

As they began to stir, I decided to bring them downstairs so we could talk. They could barely contain their excitement at having a good friend to visit at such an early hour, but finally I managed to sit them down. I reminded them of the mouse we had found in the garden and the discussion we had shared at that time. Then very gently I broke the news about Richard. Daddy had gone. He wouldn't be coming back, not today, not later, not ever. He had died. He had left his body behind and was now in heaven with Jesus. I knew they wouldn't be able to take it all in yet, especially the one-year-old. I was struggling with it myself, but it was a start. I had crossed the first hurdle, and life would go on.

The moment did not last long, and soon the children were clamouring for their breakfast and wanting to play. My mind struggled to focus on what to do next. Getting breakfast seemed like the easiest thing to do, and so I busied myself with the normal things, leaving my thoughts to wander where they willed. I decided to go up to our bedroom, my bedroom now. I did not want the children to be disturbed by finding it in a state, so I quickly tidied up and changed the bed before I showered and put on fresh clothes. It was good to wash off the traces of my exertion and the smell of the hospital from my skin.

My mind felt so full of half-joined thoughts, each one screaming louder than the previous one in an effort to be heard. I was a widow. What exactly did that mean? I had no clue. My mind flitted to the house; it was tied to Richard's job. Would I soon be homeless? I suddenly remembered the wedding that Richard had been due to conduct later that day; how would I break it to the couple that their vicar had died? And how would I get in touch with them anyway? I needed to let the clergy team know, but it was still too early to ring. The family, his and mine, I wanted to be the first to know, but I could not call them at this unearthly hour. And how would I find the words to tell them that Richard had died? I tried to stay busy to keep the pain at bay until a reasonable hour.

Shortly after eight I began the long round of calls. I was grateful that there was someone else to help me with the children and that I had already managed to give the news to them. My mind went back to lectures at medical school on how to break bad news, and with each telling it became a little easier as the reality sank in a little more. I was now a widow. I had passed to the other side of married, and had exited the door. How rudely I had been pushed into the next chapter of my life, and how harshly the blow had fallen. My greatest nightmare had come true. My journey into grief had begun.

2 The last goodbyes

The rest of that first day was full of activity and people. Among the first to arrive was a member of the clergy team, and I was deeply touched by her compassion and grace. Other friends of Richard's came too, people I hardly knew, dropping everything to be with me, and proving themselves to be true friends in my hour of need. The husband of the friend who had come in the night arrived, bringing their boys with him. He was visibly shaken, and seeing him so stricken helped me to release some of my pain. Then came the bishop, to reassure me of his care.

I seemed to spend all morning moving from one group of people to the next, going over the events of the night again and again, while trying to create some sense of normality for myself by pegging the washing on the line. It was a brilliantly sunny morning, and I appreciated being able to be outside where the temperature was warm. Inside I still had the sense of icy coldness that had descended upon me in the hospital, and an immense feeling of tiredness that hung like a thick fog over all I did.

In the middle of all this activity, some dear friends from the Midlands rang unexpectedly to ask if they could visit, being as yet completely unaware of my situation. Gladly I accepted their offer before telling them my devastating news, and they arrived just as the crowds were beginning to thin out. It felt good to be with those who had known and loved me for a long time, and although I knew that my own family would have willingly come, I feared that their own grief would be too much for me to bear.

After a simple lunch together we headed into town. I needed to get away from the claustrophobic feel of the house, and to escape from the telephone for a while to begin to process my thoughts and unwind. My friends listened graciously as my jumbled thoughts poured out.

As they prepared to leave, someone else arrived with a cooked meal. I gratefully fed the children before getting them ready for bed. The quietness of the house was just starting to descend on me when the doorbell rang again. Another good friend had driven two hours or more just to be with us tonight and reassure us of her family's love and care. Reluctantly I let her go, recognizing that I needed some time on my own, but knowing that the silence of the house would now envelop me. The day had been so long. As I wound my way wearily upstairs, the sight of the empty bed made me gasp in pain. There would be no loving embrace to end the day with now, and no-one with whom to pray. I felt so vulnerable and alone. I turned my thoughts to God, knowing that he was the only one who could help me through.

As soon as I awoke the next morning, I was hit by a dense wall of pain. The bed was cold and empty on Richard's side, and I found myself reliving the events of the morning before. I didn't want it to be true, but there was no escape. Richard had not come back, and I had left his body on a cold hospital trolley to be wheeled away to the morgue. A hard balloon of grief seemed to inflate itself in my stomach and chest, making it difficult for me to breathe.

The children were now waking up and so I busied myself with the usual routine, not sure what else to do. It was

Sunday, and I needed to go to church. I wanted to keep things as normal as possible for the children and for myself, but I did not really appreciate how painful it might be for me to walk through those doors. I was wading through a sea of numbness and tears, and my only thought was to keep going as best I could.

As we arrived at church there was an almost audible gasp. It seemed that no-one had anticipated that we would come. Not everyone had heard the news yet, and I watched as various people were taken to one side. There was a general announcement too from the front, and I did my best to meet the vast array of eyes that inevitably turned my way. All I could think about was getting through, and I didn't really care whether I laughed or cried. The wall of pain that had hit me as we entered the church was excruciating, and I knew that it would be a long time until it would subside.

I escaped as soon as I could, glad that another hurdle had been cleared, but uncertain what the rest of the day would bring. The house seemed so barren and devoid of comfort as we returned, knowing that there would be no-one to follow us home. The day stretched ahead like a gaping void without Richard, and I was unsure how I would manage to get through. I fought back the tears as I removed his place setting from the table and tried to spread out our seats as much as I could to hide the gap. The pain burned into my consciousness like a searing hot iron. How could I face Richard's absence day after day after day? Would the pain always be this bad? My eyes were red and sore from crying, and I was weary beyond belief. I begged God to give me the energy to see me through the day as I limped on with our normal routine.

Thankfully it was not long before another set of visitors arrived, this time with children in tow. It was good to hear laughter ring out once again as the children romped around the house and jumped up eagerly to receive hugs and cuddles from the adult guests. I had to smile at their ability to enjoy life even in the midst of great pain.

Another meal appeared as a spontaneous gift, with the promise of more over the next few weeks. I gratefully accepted, knowing I could not cope with cooking just yet. Simply getting through the day intact was arduous enough.

Along with the meals came gifts of shopping, and baskets of ironing were taken and returned. There were so many offers of help that it was hard to keep track. I waded my way through the remaining phone calls and tried to work out what to do next. I was anxious to keep life running as smoothly as possible for the children, and so we attended our usual toddler groups out of routine. At least there the children would get some play time away from the reminders of Richard's death, and the monotony of the day would be relieved.

Everywhere I went I was faced by pitying looks as people tried to understand what I was going through. I didn't want to have to explain my story over and over again, and yet it was inevitable that people wanted to speak to me. I did my best to cope with their well-meaning comments, and Sellotaped a wan smile on to my face to cover my pain. The wound was too raw and too fresh as yet for me to share it with anyone.

The shock and numbness that had begun at the hospital had now completely enveloped me, and I felt as if my emotions were suspended somewhere in mid-air. The pain was pressed so close to my heart, with very little room left to breathe, but I dared not begin to process my feelings just yet. There was a funeral to organize and still more people to tell, as well as the issue of getting used to dealing with everything on my own. Ruefully I found myself feeling glad that I had previously done so much of the childcare myself; at least that was familiar territory to me.

The days swung between feeling utterly normal as I faced the tasks I had always done, and feeling as if I had been dumped in some strange and barren landscape with few signposts. Each new hurdle I attempted simply added to the pain I felt inside, and yet I kept it all in, too scared to release it in any way. Decisions had to be made regarding undertakers and disposing of Richard's body, and various agencies had to be informed. Visitors came and went with dizzying speed, and the phone calls seemed incessant. I lurched from one decision to the next, grateful when others showed me the way through.

Expressions of sympathy started to pour in by mail, as well as letters that had to be opened on Richard's behalf. And there were so many flowers, a beautiful but poignant reminder of what had just taken place and the gaping void inside. All I wanted was for Richard to come back through the door. I would hear a car in the driveway and start expectantly, and then the realization would hit me afresh: he would not be coming home any more. I would walk past his study and have to stifle a groan. There would be no more glimpses of him in there.

As I floundered through the first few days, I was aware of another hurdle that had to be overcome. A post mortem needed to be completed, something that seemed to hit delay upon delay. Pictures of Richard's body lying on a cold marble slate ready to be prised open and examined in excruciating detail kept flooding my mind. It felt too much that the body that had once caressed me so lovingly would now be torn in shreds as they sought to determine why he had died. And I still had a sense of uneasiness about my resuscitation attempt. Would they blame me for his death as they cut him apart, or would I be redeemed? It was a torture I felt unable to share with anyone as I waited for news.

My mind was full of the 'why' question: why had he died? It was a question I dared not voice to anyone else for fear that it would drive me further from God. I felt sure God could take it though, and so daily I took my grief to him.

I knew there would be no answers, and suspected I would not like them if there were, but I had to let it out rather than leave it to fester within. Tears were never far from my eyes, as normal day-to-day activities brought the memories flooding back. There was no-one to call when it was meal-time, and no-one else to answer the phone. There were only three plates to serve at dinnertime, and only three jackets now hanging by the door. The future was a black hole waiting to swallow me up, and so I chose to block it out. It was enough that there was a funeral to arrange, but at least the delayed post mortem bought me some time to work things through. I felt as if I was on the pathologist's table, slowly being sliced in two and left to exsanguinate in silence and in shame.

At last the post mortem was completed and the results were released, causing my mind to reel again. Asthma was the cause, and then Richard's stomach had seemingly emptied itself into his lungs in response. How could this be? Richard's asthma had always been so well controlled. I asked to be allowed to speak to the pathologist myself, and graciously he agreed. Now I asked the question that had been plaguing my mind. Was it my fault? Had my poor resus-citation attempt been the final straw? The answer was no. And so I was able to put my mind at rest. I would never know what had happened in the moments before I awoke that fateful night, but I knew that God had been there all along. He had allowed this to happen, and I had to leave it at that. Richard's body could be released to the funeral directors, and I would be able to see him again.

Now I was under pressure to name a day for the funeral. I found it difficult to give a date for such a final act. I wanted time to grieve properly and say my goodbyes, and for me there was no rush. I wanted to see Richard's body again, to stroke his furrowed brow, and touch the places where the pathologists had gone in. I wanted to have time to let the awful reality of his death sink in before I closed this chapter of my life.

In the end I was gently pressed into making a decision, and I allowed other people to take the strain. Richard's father helped me plan the service and choose the songs. All I wanted was to be able to express my thanks to God for all the time I had shared with Richard, and to give him my heart anew. We decided to have a short family service at the crematorium first, before facing a larger, more public service of thanksgiving at the church. Three friends were asked to give short eulogies, and I found a poem to remind me not to hurry through my grief. And in between we placed songs to help us lift our eyes off our pain and on to God. As others took on the organizing, I allowed myself to be carried along by God and the prayers of those around.

But before all that could happen, I needed to view Richard's body as it was now. I steeled myself for what I would find, but nothing could prepare me for the shock of seeing him so cold and yellow and still, in a deep, white-lined coffin on a stand. I felt unnerved by the eerie silence as I gazed at him in the flickering candlelight. His face was so swollen and bruised, with beads of moisture on his brow, and the clothes he wore hung awkwardly around his rigid frame. The stitches from the post mortem, although largely hidden from sight, looked like barbs of wire lancing his skin. Somehow it felt dishonest looking at him through such soft, dim light, and I almost wished I had seen him in the hospital morgue. I did not want anyone else to see him in this state, and I wasn't sure I would have the strength to return.

My daughter, however, was struggling to understand how Daddy had left his body behind, and seemed to have suddenly hit the 'why?' stage. I laughed at God's sense of humour, allowing this childhood phase to arrive just now, and reluctantly I took her to see Richard's battered frame. A moment was all she needed to convince herself that Daddy had gone.

The funeral was now approaching fast, and the next hurdle was to find an outfit for me to wear. I felt utterly lost going clothes shopping without Richard, and the thought of buying an outfit alone for such a public occasion filled me with fear. A good friend steadied my nerves as the children ran in between the rails. God was gracious, and before long I had found an olive green trouser suit to wear with a red top underneath. I did not want to don the black garb of a widow just yet, and the bright colour of the top peeping out helped to remind me of Richard's love of colourful things and make me smile.

The funeral took place almost two weeks after Richard's death. I busied myself playing with the children while the last-minute preparations were being made, trying to keep things as normal as possible for as long as I could. But just as we were leaving the house, I crashed into something hard. A huge egg began to swell above my eye. I didn't have time to stop and grab some ice. I laughed ruefully to myself as I thought of my developing black eye.

The journey in the limousine behind the coffin was agonizing in the extreme, as I nursed my fractured thoughts and my bruised head. I tried to avoid looking at the hearse and concentrate on the children instead, desperately praying that the ordeal would not prove to be too much for them.

The service at the crematorium did little to assuage the torture I felt. I struggled to sing in the unfamiliar environment, and found it utterly hideous looking at the coffin ahead. I wanted to be alone in my grief, and hug it to me to stop the pain, as I struggled to accept that I would never see Richard's body again. I tried to block out the other people in the room, and say my own goodbyes. I hung back as the service came to an end, wanting to be the final one to leave, and placed a single rose upon the wood before the curtains closed. It was over, and yet it had barely begun.

I said nothing as we were transported to the church, hoping I would feel more comfortable there. I could not begin to express how empty and desolate I felt. But as we arrived, I had to stifle a cry of dismay. I had not anticipated such a crowd. The church was packed to capacity and beyond. Resolutely I followed the bishop to our seats near the front, doing my best to ignore the sea of faces on the way. The desire to escape into the sunshine outside was strong, but I fixed my eyes on the front of the church, glad that I had no vocal role to play. All I wanted was to worship God as best I could, no matter how bad the pain, and to offer him my life again.

Through my throbbing headache and whirring thoughts, I barely heard the words the bishop spoke. I felt detached as others spoke in praise of a man I thought I had known so well, and yet had barely begun to understand. I felt ashamed that I had not been able to appreciate his gifts for what they were, and angry that he had left me to cope all alone. Willingly I gave God my broken heart, knowing that only he had the power to make it whole.

Finally the service came to an end and slowly I made my way down to the hall, longing for a corner in which to hide. But the fact that Richard's story had been emblazoned across the front page of the local press just a few days ago meant that I was public property now. I found myself being swamped by a long procession of well-wishers, some of whom I barely knew. At least I could laugh with them about the colourful bump above my eye; this was far preferable to opening up my wounded heart.

As the queue dispersed, my close friends and family surrounded me on every side. I felt honoured that they cared so very much, and had driven so far to be with me today. And yet I found it hard that they could return to their lives as usual tonight, while I would be struggling on alone.

Eventually it was time to go. I gratefully accepted the offer of a lift home with some members of Richard's family, feeling somehow closer to him because of it. We chatted for a short while outside as the last rays of sunshine left the sky, before they too left for their homes.

The day ended as quietly as it had begun, with just the three of us in the vicarage on our own. I was exhausted from the emotional charge of the day, and unable or unwilling to look beyond bedtime for what tomorrow would bring.

3 The journey begins

The flurry of activity that had led up to the 'big day' was now gone, and there was no longer anything towards which to aim. It was hard not to feel abandoned as the future stretched out ahead. People were slowly returning to the normality of their lives, and expecting me to return to mine. But what had been normal was no more, and I had to work out how to go on. The pain was returning with a vengeance as the numbness and shock wore off, and I felt lost and terribly isolated in the unfamiliar territory of my grief. I had never experienced pain this relentless or intense before, a cold sharp pain that gripped my insides with a ferocity that left me panting for breath. I was terrified of what it would do to me if I let it take control as its fierce teeth seemed to be ripping through my outer defences with alarming speed. I groped forward, anxious and forlorn. Where was it taking me, and when would it spit me out?

The gaping void which Richard had filled ached physically within me as I tried to drag myself through each day. Everything was an effort, and I felt as if I was carrying a huge weight. Routines became my saviour. I could see only as far as the next meal, and even that was a strain. I counted the hours until bedtime when I could legitimately turn out the light. The days were dark and lonesome, and I felt as if I was clawing my way through on hands and knees.

Life had been hard enough looking after two little ones before Richard had died; now that difficulty had hit an altogether different magnitude as I struggled with my own feelings of loss while trying not to add to their pain.

I poured myself into my mothering as if to anaesthetize myself from my inner torment. But new hurdles were arising all the time as the children developed, and it was hard having no-one around to share them with. I was constantly wading through a sea of tears, with little hope of finding the shore.

Food still stuck in my gullet, but I did my best to eat, knowing that I needed to keep my strength up for the long grind ahead. I swung from moments of lucidity when things seemed much as they had always been, to moments of utter despair that life would never be enjoyable again.

It was July and that meant I had to negotiate our wedding anniversary alone. How that stung. I kept myself busy in a vain attempt to block out the pain, and soldiered on. It felt too hard that I could not celebrate with Richard by going for a long walk in the countryside or sharing a special meal at home, as we had so often done.

As the summer holidays loomed, I realized I could not face going away for long, and so I chose to stay at home, grateful that many of the memories around the town were ones I had forged alone. Dear friends took us on day trips and invited us round, and I made as many excuses as I could to keep us busy. But at the same time as needing to give myself distance from all the places that reminded me of Richard, perversely I also longed to be close to him again, and so I found myself deliberately seeking out places full of memories of him.

Nervously I ventured to my father-in-law's flat an hour's drive away, hoping that our shared grief might bring some solace to my battered soul. But the area where he lived had been an old stomping ground where the memories of Richard were still overwhelmingly strong. Valiantly I fought back the tears as I remembered the tender moments we had shared when our relationship was still young, and I desperately sought to erase the recollections of happy times with friends. The result was that I returned home even more exhausted than before.

I felt compelled to visit other places too where I could remember Richard: locations that we had enjoyed exploring together and beautiful countryside that we had driven through. Sometimes I would enlist the help of special friends to enable me to build new memories to lessen the pain. With each hurdle thus cleared, I would feel a strange sense of satisfaction, but inevitably those days ended in tears as I allowed myself to feel the full ferocity of my pain.

As the term began and the children's groups resumed, I threw myself into finding a new routine for us all. I was so grateful that the children provided me with a purpose to get through each day and gave me so many reasons to smile. I clung to them, seeing in my motherhood a reason to go on. I wanted them to be able to play as much as possible, and so I tried to provide as many outlets as I could for them to have fun. It seemed easier when we were out and about, and so I planned numerous trips to the local parks and shops to fill our time. But going out so regularly had a different pain attached: it still hurt each time we came back through those doors to find an empty house where nothing had changed.

Underneath the outward flurry of activity, I longed for space just to sit quietly and absorb the terrible nature of my loss, but I could not let myself sit still. To do so would be to invite the tears to begin, and I feared that once they started I would never persuade them to stop. Instead play dates were arranged for the children, providing them and me with company. But it was not always easy, as I found it hard to talk about how I was getting on.

I was desperate to be seen to be coping as I muddled my way along, and so I rarely chose to talk about what lay within. Instead I preferred to focus on the children and how they were developing. Beneath the surface I was all too well aware of the unending sea of pain that was my grief, and the bubbles of anger that so often found their way to the top. The only respite I could allow myself was two afternoons a week when the children were cared for in a nursery, a standing arrangement from the days when I had worked as a GP. I knew I could not face that work just now with my inner resources so stretched, and so I reluctantly accepted the sick notes my doctor issued and stayed away.

But the silence of the house on those two afternoons was even more devastating, knowing that the children were away from me. The thought of being alone filled me with dread, a fear of what I might find in the dark emptiness within. And knowing I could not even spend this time with Richard made the pain sting still more.

Looking back, I could see that I had relied on Richard far too much, been dependent on him almost. Now the support I had built my life around had collapsed, and I was surveying the wreckage. Superficially I looked as if I was coping, but underneath I was weeping day after day after day. I no longer knew who I was as a person in my own right, and the emptiness inside was threatening to destroy me.

Only when I was alone could I allow myself to acknowledge my pain, and unwind a little bit more. Gradually my time alone became a refuge, a place to shelter from life's storms. The routines could only do so much to anaesthetize me from the rawness of my pain. I knew I needed to let it all go, and so I sought the warmth of God's love, desperate to feel it in a very tangible way. Those afternoons began to provide me with an ideal opportunity for time with him undisturbed. There in God's presence I could pour out my undiluted pain, and beg for some sign of hope as the darkness enveloped me again and again. And there I could learn to rest in his arms, safe and secure. Often I found that God would meet me where I was, offering a picture, a verse or a song of hope for me to carry into the rest of the day and give me the grace I needed.

Gradually I began to recognize that the time I had on my own was precious indeed. I began to respect my space by cordoning it off, declining to answer the doorbell or phone. Slowly but surely my time alone became a mini-sanctuary, a resting place, a time just to 'be' without the demands of the world pressing in. In that space I found myself wanting to sit in God's presence, to soak up his goodness and love, while I waded through my painful memories. And I eagerly devoured all the books I could find from the local Christian bookshop on grief. The reassurance they brought that my turbulent feelings were normal was huge indeed. In them I found poems and readings that gently ministered to my bruised and beaten soul, and I clung on to the promises they seemed to give that one day I would again start to feel hope. Right now the days seemed very dark indeed, and I held on to those words as little rays of light across a violent sea, as the fragile vessel of my life was tossed relentlessly to and fro.

In between the fleeting times alone, I immersed myself in my motherhood again. At least I could function on that level, and make it to the end of each day. My sense of self was too shaky, too fragile to be exposed, and I hid behind the only role I felt I had left. I crept my way forward day by day, hardly daring to look at what the future might hold, and barely letting the children out of my sight. A great heaviness had descended upon my body, and every step felt as if it were uphill. Planning ahead was simply not possible just now. I felt as if my life had been severed in two, leaving a raw and gaping wound that I carried with me whatever I did. The nerve endings had been left flapping in the breeze, and even the lightest touch or comment left me reeling in agony.

The only other role that seemed available to me was my job. Previously I had enjoyed the mental stimulation it brought as I spent time away from the children, and better days tried to convince me that I was strong enough to return. But I felt so drained and devoid of energy that I knew deep down I could not take the plunge just yet.

It was now almost six months since Richard had died, and although I had dealt with many of the 'firsts', there were quite a few still to go. I decided to do Christmas differently from previous years when we had been tied by Richard's job. We went again to my father-in-law's flat along with other members of Richard's family, wanting to be near those who had loved him so much. I focused on cooking the Christmas meal on my own, using it as an excuse to keep my turbulent emotions at bay, all the time knowing that they would return in full force at the end of the day.

The next hurdle was my birthday, and I chose to spend it with friends. I did my best to forget the beautiful meal that Richard had cooked for me the year before, and the comment he had made to the friends we had shared it with that he could not imagine himself ever growing old. Overall it seemed as if the pain was growing steadily with each month, and I was not sure how much longer I could go on.

March brought the next anniversary to overcome: Richard's birthday, a 'first' that filled me with dread. How could I celebrate in his absence? And yet I knew I had to mark the day somehow. As usual I employed the trick of keeping myself as busy as I could in an attempt to take the edge off the harshness of the pain, and chose to bake a special cake that we could all enjoy.

But as spring wore on, it felt as if the rawness of my grief was returning with a vengeance. My sleep was becoming increasingly erratic and my appetite had started to wane. Knowing we were on the home straight as far as first anniversaries were concerned did little to lift my mood, and I found myself being irritable and angry much of the time. The strain of the last year was beginning to show, and life felt barren and desolate. Each day it felt as if I were gritting my teeth simply to get through, and laughter was all but absent from my life as my mood plummeted and my concentration dipped. I turned to God again, not knowing what else to do. If anyone could get me through, then it was him. All I could do was offer him my pain once more, and surrender it all to him.

Easter was now almost upon us, and I was feeling restless and anxious to move on. It seemed as if I was falling into a pit of despair, with no guarantee that I would ever get out.

I decided it would be good to get away, so we went to stay with some dear friends for the Easter weekend. This did the trick and gave us a much-needed mini-break, but once again I was plunged into emotional exhaustion when we returned home.

I felt I had no reserves left as I approached the children's birthdays. The pain in my heart was throbbing constantly, and I felt incredibly afraid. I clung on to a picture I was given of me huddled in a boat with Jesus at the helm, allowing him to steer me confidently through the tempestuous sea.

Then out of the blue I received a phone call from work requesting an urgent meeting. Reluctantly I gave up my afternoon alone and went in, totally oblivious to the shock that I was about to receive. It was now almost a year since I had been there, and during that time they had showed me the utmost consideration and care, even continuing to pay me for much of that time. Now they had come to the conclusion that they could not hold my post open any longer, and I would have to go. I was stunned. What I had thought was going to be a nice little chat about how I was getting on and an opportunity to unload some of my pain had turned into yet another nightmare scenario. I was out of work. I managed to be gracious enough to thank them for all they had done for me, and then raced home.

I could no longer contain the tears. They simply poured out of me hour after hour as I curled myself up tightly into a ball. It was too much. I could not go on. Not only had I lost my role as a wife, I had lost my role as a doctor too. There was no use in pretending I was coping any longer, and I was forced to accept that I needed help. My understanding GP put me on to antidepressants to try to ease the strain. My life was in tatters, and I felt naked and exposed.

The week-long May bank holiday now lay ahead, and I decided to go back to my father-in-law's flat, desperate to feel close to Richard again.

I made it through the hour's drive intact, praying for strength and concentration all the way, and waited expectantly outside his flat to be let in. But as the moments passed and there was no reply, my stomach began to churn. No message had been left for us, nor had John been seen, and so the warden accompanied us upstairs, uncertain and concerned. Quickly I raced on ahead, desperate to find John first, hoping the children would be okay for a time with a member of staff downstairs.

I found him lying on the bathroom floor, barely conscious and freezing cold. It seemed that he had collapsed in the night and lain there, unable to get to the cord to call for help. My mind did not want to take this in. I covered him with a blanket and phoned 999. Valiantly I pushed my overstretched emotions to one side, and tried to take control. I rang a good friend to come and sit with the children, unsure what would be required of me next.

As the ambulance crew arrived, I hung back, not knowing what else to do. I just could not face accompanying my father-in-law to the hospital in an ambulance right now. Alarm bells were ringing in my head, and I knew I needed some space. The children were getting hungry, and we all needed to eat. Hastily we grabbed some food before heading on to the hospital to meet Grandpa. I was relieved to see that his condition had improved, and that he was sitting up and able to talk through the oxygen mask on his face. My heart rate began to slow down, and I was able to take the children to say hello. Wearily I made my way back to his flat, thankful that things were turning out all right after all, and got the children ready for bed before telephoning Richard's siblings scattered far and wide.

My friend had just gone home when the telephone rang again. It was the hospital. John had taken a sudden turn for the worse and had been moved to the intensive care unit. I had to go. I called my friend, asking her to return, and hastily rang round John's children again, knowing that they would want to come despite the distances involved. Some kind family friends came to take me across town and stayed with me as I began a long night of vigil in intensive care. This was the night of vigil I never had with Richard, when his life was so suddenly expunged.

I spent the night alternating between John's bedside and a side room while waiting for more news. I did my best to concentrate on the present, but my mind was elsewhere, thrown back to that fateful night in June 2004. Going through it again was gruelling, and I could hardly bear to let myself think about, let alone feel, what was going on inside.

As the night wore on, the first of John's children arrived and urged me to go back and rest. But I knew I would not manage to sleep. I had come this far with him, and could not walk out now. However, as more of John's children gathered, I knew my presence was no longer required. My own children would soon be awake, and I needed to be with them.

My father-in-law's flat was now full of various family members who had arrived in the night with children in tow. My children awoke, happy to see their cousins, but surprised by the news. I decided to take them to the unit while I could, anxious that they have a chance this time to say goodbye.

The hushed environment, the noisy machines and the profusion of tubes coming from John's body gave rise to many questions as the children attempted to take it all in. I did not want to frighten them by what they saw, but thought it might help them process their grief for Richard and give them a chance to ask the questions they had been unable to articulate before. My eyes were full of tears as we walked away, leaving John's children to surround him as he made his way home to join his wife, and Richard, his first-born son, later that day.

Another role, that of daughter-in-law, had been stripped away, and once again I was writhing in acute pain. Where had I gone wrong? I had done all I could to help him, and could not blame myself. I was glad we had been there that day, and had to see God's hand at work in the timing of it all. But the pain was excruciating, and the future looked impenetrably black. There would be another funeral to go to, within a few days of the anniversary of Richard's death. What had been intended as an enjoyable holiday had turned into another nightmare to be endured. The family huddled around me to shut out the cold I felt so keenly inside, assuring me of their love and concern, as I groped my way through the darkest black of night. Desolate felt too weak a word for what I was experiencing. I was utterly devastated and numb.

Desperately I reached for my role of motherhood again, not knowing what else to do. Life was careering violently out of control, and I felt as if I was being buffeted mercilessly by sky-high waves. All I could do was pray that God would guide me through these rough deep waters and see me through to the other side. My nerves felt frayed to utter rawness.

My sense of value and worth lay in tatters and I no longer knew who I was beneath the carnage of my life. I realized too late that I had idolized the roles I had played with such vigour, and they had become false gods to me, trusting in them rather than in my Maker and his love for me.

This had not been done intentionally, of course, but somehow over the years I had slipped easily into a daily mode of operating that had pushed God aside. Years of neglect meant that the inner me, my very self, was barely there, and it needed resuscitating fast.

I knew that the roles I had played had not been intrinsically bad; rather it was the way I had chosen to live through them that had resulted in this mess. It was my dependence on them that had become a source of sin, getting between me and God, something he was now showing me quite clearly, and with much gentleness. Again the tears flowed freely, as I confessed my sin to him and allowed him to lead me on. I had to learn a new way of 'being' that would enable the authentic me to come alive. I had to learn afresh that my sense of value and worth came from God's love for me and who I was in him, and not from what I was doing or what role I was seeking to play. I was God's child, a product of his creation, and there alone my identity lay.

4 Traps and pitfalls

A great sense of desolation and dislocation now descended upon me as I dealt with this fresh blow. I knew that within my own family I was secure, and that they would support me constantly, even though they lived some distance away, but my position within the Fair family felt shaky in the extreme. I felt guilty that I had been the one to find John collapsed on the floor, but I backed away from accepting the blame; I had been too close to that before. Instead I bottled up my feelings even more as I crawled my way through each day. Any sense of achievement I might have felt at getting through my first year of widowhood intact was completely overshadowed by this newer and fresher grief.

The Fair family were amazing, giving me repeated assurances of their continued love and support, and they bent over backwards to make me feel as if I was still of value to them all. But I found it hard to accept that they would still want me around, and watched myself withdrawing from them more and more. I was too full of my own grief even to want to try to understand what they were going through as they began to sort John's possessions and share them out. My mind was overwhelmed with the magnitude of the 'why' questions once again, and I sank deeper and deeper into myself. Why had all this happened to me now, when I was still barely standing after Richard's death? Why had I been abandoned by God in this way? I felt angry and confused. Once again I allowed a blanket of numbness to cocoon me from my pain. I did not want to face the sharp edges of my grief that seemed to protrude from under its protection, fearing that I would shatter into a thousand pieces at one touch. I found myself watching as if from a distance as plans were made for the funeral, and as the aftermath of John's death took its toll.

I resented the fact that all the conversation now seemed to be about John. I was desperate for some mention of Richard's name. I hid behind my lack of feeling as the funeral took place, opting instead for the relatively straightforward task of occupying the children as they played around my feet.

After the service was over, many of the family stayed around for a few days, using the opportunity to catch up with one another and sort out John's flat. Yet again, I hid behind the children rather than face up to the pain within. I felt I had no right to be there, and struggled with the family's insistence that I still had a place in their hearts. I could not bring myself to request anything as John's belongings were shared around, despite repeated urgings from the family to speak up, and I found it hard to accept the few things that were eventually pressed into my hands. I was so afraid that my position in the family would be declared null and void, and it was as if I were trying to do the rejection myself to make it easier for them if they wanted to let me go.

My feelings of loss were immense as I found myself paying many visits to the flat over the ensuing weeks, as if to absorb the magnitude of my loss in a more gradual way. Not only had I lost a vital connection to Richard, I had also lost my bolt-hole in the town of my youth, the place that was so full of reminiscences of Richard-and-Janine when we had first met. How I grieved for the memories that were tied up there, as furniture that had been in place for years was gradually taken away. How I hurt when the pictures were stripped from the walls, leaving only an empty shell behind. It felt like a symbol of what had happened to my life where so many things had been torn away. Not surprisingly, I found myself slipping further and further into a pit of despair. The anger that had been fermenting inside was pulling me down, and I seemed to be spiralling ever more quickly into a haze of self-pity and bitterness.

Even on the very first morning of my grief I had recognized that bitterness and self-pity would be a particular temptation to me. The recent events I was now struggling to accept had given me the excuse I needed to wallow in my pain. I felt justified in feeling angry inside when I had been left to deal with so much agony alone. I felt bitter about how I had been treated through the long months of my grief so far when friends had apparently abandoned me. I was frustrated with my constant lack of progress and persistent low mood. And I was livid with myself for requiring medication simply to survive, and for falling down the slippery slope of despair.

Depression was an old friend of mine, one I would rather not have re-met. My emotions felt utterly turbulent as the battle raged within. Waves of hopelessness washed over me as I abandoned myself to my grief, leaving me feeling even more wretched and dejected. Exhaustion threatened to overtake me, and I knew I had to slow down. But still I chose to continue with the relentless pace I had set myself, in an attempt simply to get through.

It seemed that the children were suffering too, and that compounded my own agony. The novelty of going to Grandpa's flat to sort things out was wearing thin, and I was constantly frazzled and short-tempered with them. I longed for space to sort myself out, to fall apart even, but worried that there would be no-one there to pick up the pieces if I should fall. My faith in God seemed far too fragile to withstand this storm as I feebly sought to cling on to him, knowing he was the only one who could bring me through.

And I was no longer sure whom I was grieving for. The pain had increased to such a pitch that it seemed to be one overwhelming amorphous mass, the different aspects of which were indistinguishable from the whole. I found myself groaning in agony, with groans so deep that there were no longer any words adequate to describe it.

My resentment and anger boiled over again as people who had not spoken to me for months came forward on the first anniversary of Richard's death. I knew they didn't really want to hear how I was doing right now, and I wasn't sure I would tell them if they did. Instead I plastered a false smile on to my face and gave them the answer they seemed to require, that I was okay, and I had made it through the first year intact.

But denying the reality of what was going on within only served to fuel my anger even more. I felt like a hypocrite and a liar as I lashed out at the children day after day. Each minor misdemeanour seemed to aggravate my pain, and while I managed to keep a lid on things in public by and large, in the privacy of my own home I was very aware that I was raising my voice far too much. I felt ashamed that I could not cope with what was happening to me. I clung on to my times alone with God, desperate for some word of encouragement from him, some indication that things would soon get better. But instead I felt an impending sense of doom, as if some new disaster were about to strike.

A fresh round of goodbyes then needed to be made as friends left the area for good. I found myself barely able to acknowledge their departure, feeling far too sensitive to loss of any kind. Then the clergywoman who had offered me such compassion, friendship and grace throughout the long journey of my grief came to the end of her job. How I hurt inside. I could not bring myself to go to her leaving service for fear that I would curl up and die.

A wave of grief ripped through my tortured soul as I realized afresh all I had lost in Richard. My role of clergy wife, the one I had longed to fulfil even before I had met Richard all those years ago, had been snatched from me. I no longer had any standing in the eyes of the church. I felt like a waste product of the system.

Yet more bitterness seemed to consume me as I wallowed. It felt unjust that I had spent so much time intertwining my life around Richard's and investing so much energy in supporting him in his role. Now that it had all been wrenched away, the ache was too unbearable for words. As I wrestled with these issues, I became less comfortable around my clergy friends. Their presence and their clerical clothing riled me as I struggled to know how to react. I no longer had a place among their number, and missed being in the inner ring as information was exchanged. Now I had to rely on others to tell me what was happening, and work out how to respond, alone.

It felt too strange simply going back to being another parishioner, especially in a place where the only identity I had known was that of vicar's wife. The feeling of spiritual homelessness was great, and I knew that one day I would have to move on. I did not want to burden the church further by sharing my grief, for I knew they themselves were reeling. And I worried that my continued presence at that church might act as a stumbling block and prevent them from dealing with their own pain. The taste of bitterness grew more appealing as I nursed my bruised emotions week after week.

Further goodbyes came along as my daughter left the playgroup she had attended since before Richard's death. Yet another link with Richard was being torn away, and I was being forced to move on. As I made it to the first parents' evening at the school she would shortly attend, I felt wretched, and conspicuously alone.

And then more friends announced they were unexpectedly moving on. Every departure seemed like an unprovoked and personal assault as I limped my way along, and my anger soared to new heights. How dare God take them away from me now, just when I needed people to be close? How could he put me through yet more anguish and pain? My self-pity was becoming utterly absorbing, as I could not see past my own nose to the fact that God was still in control.

Going to church had been a battle from the start, but now there was fresh agony as I thought of those who were no longer around. I had managed to continue going through the early days of grief when the wound was still fresh, finding comfort in the old, familiar routines. But as time wore on and the numbness receded, the pain only seemed to increase. I felt like an embarrassment, and as if I were being watched at every move. People simply did not know what to say to me. I battled with my feelings as I trudged my way to church each Sunday, bravely pushing the buggy and holding the other child by the hand as she toddled along. And I kept my emotions closely bottled up inside until I was safely back in the privacy of my own home. Then, when the children were playing happily or asleep, I would let the tears roll silently down my cheeks as if to flush out the torment within. It was so easy to slip into victim mode, and to fill my heart with self-pity once again.

In Richard I had also lost a church leader I had greatly admired. I hated looking at the place where he had once sat to lead services and seeing someone else in his place. I found it hard to sing the songs he had enjoyed so much, remembering him with his arms outstretched in praise to God. And the songs and hymns we had used at his funeral seemed to undo me inside. Every week I would grit my teeth just to get through the church doors, where the memories were still so strong and searing. It was hard to praise God in a situation where there was so much pain.

I also found myself feeling irrationally envious of Richard in his new position. It felt ridiculous to admit that I was jealous of him now, and yet there seemed no other way to put it. He had made it through to the other side. He had achieved his life's ambition, and was now free from pain. I, on the other hand, had been left to languish in a living hell, with each day bringing fresh new forms of torture to my mind. I was the one who had been left to raise our two children alone, and he had been given the easy way out.

Negotiating my own way through grief at the same time as helping the children through their loss was so tough. I was jealous of those who had companionship every day to work through their pain, and I struggled particularly when I came across those who told me they had remarried shortly into their widowhood. I envied the intimacy I imagined they had found in their new marriages, and that left me feeling cheated and raw.

A fresh onslaught of indignation began to overwhelm me as I acknowledged another loss. Good friends were now pregnant with their third child, something about which Richard and I had dreamt. Life seemed so unkind. And the fact that my pregnancies had gone so smoothly made it doubly hard to bear. Again I ranted at God about the injustices I perceived he had placed in my life.

Then there was the matter of the summer holidays, another ordeal to endure without the usual structures of groups to attend. I muddled my way through as best I could, clinging on to the two nursery afternoons for as long as I could. Once again I found myself battling within over how to use the time, especially as the holiday wore on and the jobs slowly backed up. But the war had already been won, and I knew that I needed to spend at least part of my time alone each week with God. He had been knocking on the door of my heart for some time, despite my reluctance to respond and my fear of what he would expose inside.

This summer there would also be another source of pain: a holiday for the whole Fair family which John had booked many months before. His place was filled by an aunt, and the holiday went ahead, much to the delight of the children, who wanted to see their cousins once again. I enjoyed spending time with them all away from the intensity of sorting out John's flat, and was relieved to find that the friendships that had grown between myself and various family members before Richard had died still seemed to be intact.

Nevertheless, it was another acutely painful experience. The area where we stayed held many associations with Richard, as it was one that we had often explored together. I wished he was there again as I wiggled my way around the country roads to some of our favourite haunts, half expecting to see him there. And I threw myself into the role of tour guide when I could, wanting to put my local knowledge to good use and distract myself from the pain.

As the summer holidays came to an end, there was yet another goodbye. The nursery my children had attended for so long was no longer viable for me and I had to let it go. The downside was that my time alone was reduced, as the new school routine coupled with the new playgroup I had found for my son meant shorter afternoons. Once again a cry of 'It's not fair' rose to my lips as self-pity reared its ugly head, closely followed by bitterness, jealousy and despair. Now more than ever I knew I needed to spend some time alone with God; it was the only way I would cope with the new changes, and I hoped that this limited time would be enough to offer me some sort of balance as I careered aimlessly through life.

I longed for some sort of reassurance that I was doing okay, and yet I knew that I was still attempting to deny the reality of my grief. I had spent the summer simply getting through, and although the numbness of my grief had worn off again, I had done my best to push the pain away. I was scared of entering into its darkness, not knowing where it might lead, and so I had fallen into the trap of using self-pity, bitterness, jealousy and despair to make a thin veneer to keep me from delving within.

It seemed as if God was getting restless with my persistent attempts to keep him at bay, and he wanted to break through. As I spent time with him, I was increasingly aware that if I wanted to keep calling him Lord, then I had to respond. I knew that I was finding it difficult to surrender myself to him, and to give him my pain, fancying that if I did not hold on to it firmly enough, my very self would collapse and die. Now I began to see that I had been using my agony to hide from him over and over again. I began to pour out my frustrations, knowing that he was big enough to take it all, and ask him to give me the courage and the will I needed to go on. I could not even surrender to him in my own strength, and needed to ask for his help simply to allow him to come in.

The corruptness of my heart overwhelmed me as I found the putrid stench of my anger spilling out. My journal was filled with pages of fury as raw emotions poured on to the page. I was appalled at what was coming from my heart, as God stirred up the murky waters deep within. This wasn't what I had bargained for at all. I had expected solace and reassurance, but God was clearly showing me that I had much repentance to do. He was not impressed with my continued reluctance to deal with the unhealthy emotions that raged within. I had spent too long looking for affirmation from others rather than looking to him.

Gently he was showing me that my heart was full of bitterness that was blocking his ability to work in me, and it seemed as if his eyes were as full of tears as mine. I could not keep expressing my desire to be more like him if I was not prepared for some radical surgery. I needed to recognize that the feelings of despair that had threatened to overwhelm me were basically a sign that he was unable or unwilling to act. The weeds of bitterness that implied that he was not able to redeem all things had to be cut out before they took a hold of my whole life, and the self-pity that I had been holding close to my heart and using to push him away was something that simply had to go.

As for the jealousy of Richard's position now and the perceived injustice of being unable to have any more children, then they did not honour God in the least. He wanted the whole of me, and not just some tiny part. He wanted me to admit my brokenness and come to him just as I was, and allow him to hold my heart. The pictures he had given me some time before of him bandaging up my brokenness and pain could only happen if I was willing to let go. I had no right to have a pain-free existence, and no right to a trouble-free life. I did not even have a right to life itself.

I needed to acknowledge that he alone was God, and allow him to be in control. I needed to know that he did not make mistakes, and all that had happened to me was within his greater plan. I needed to stop praying for the difficulties to cease, and stop seeing their continued presence as an excuse to wallow in self-pity and despair. Instead I needed to pray for strength, grace and courage to see me through until he saw fit to lift the burden. He would not guarantee that my anguish would cease at once, nor would he make things easy for me overnight, but I could trust him in this because he was God, I was his child and he loved me. He alone would provide.

I was stunned and chastened as I bent my head in shame. For so long I had tried to put myself in charge, to struggle on through each torment in my own strength and not his. I had been giving mere lip service to his lordship, and now I had to submit to his knife. The blackness still surrounded me day and night, but now I knew without a doubt that he was with me through it all. I begged for his forgiveness and asked for his help to go on.

I had spent so long lashing out at those who, unaware of what was going on inside, had plied me with pitying looks and comments. I had not wanted to accept the role of victim that their pity had seemed to imply, and instead of seeing where the trouble really lay, inside my heart, I had blamed it all on them. Likewise, I had judged those who seemed to have taken the road of bitterness after life had dealt them a harsh blow, seeing my desire to walk through my grief in a wholesome way as far superior to their feeble attempts. By doing so, I had neglected to remove the pernicious roots of bitterness from my own life and had thus allowed them to grow. The jealousy that had seemed so appropriate and right as I revelled in knowing where Richard had gone had become a millstone around my neck, and the despair that had been my excuse not to move on and grow had been exposed as a lie.

The incisions were deep and painful as God cut through the dross, and asked me to surrender it all to him. He did not want me falling into the pitfalls of my grief. He wanted more for me than that. He wanted me to trust in him and know that he was near. The scenery outside still looked incredibly bleak, but inside the light was beginning to dawn.

To keep me going I let music fill the house, and sought out all the songs of lament I could find. I could identify with the outrage expressed in the psalms, and knew that God would understand. I carefully marked out all the passages in my Bible that seemed to offer me hope, and wrote down verses that spoke directly to me, plastering them on the kitchen walls where I would see them often and remember that he cared.

My sister-in-law sent me a book called *Beauty from Ashes* by Jennifer Rees Larcombe. This felt like balm to my battered soul and ministered to me deeply, reminding me through Bible readings from Isaiah 46 and 54 that God was my husband now, and that I could look to him to provide. He would show me a way through the wastelands of my life, and bring me into a future full of promise and hope.

But often all I could do was to pour out my pain and brokenness to God, and ask for his help to go on. I clung to the verses I had found about his plans for me, plans to give me a future and a hope (Romans 8:28 and Jeremiah 29:11), and I looked at them as often as I could. It was like taking medicine for my spirit, and I had to do it regularly if it were to have its full effects. Slowly I began to see that all he was asking of me right now was that I give him my agony and allow him to carry it. He was not expecting me to shoulder the burden alone; this had never been his intention. Instead he was offering me the chance to partner with him, to give him the frustrations and the anger and the pain, and to leave them in his capable hands. He was more than able to take the weight, and I could do no better than to trust him.

It was a painful realization that I had been reluctant to accept: I was empty and had nothing to bring except my fractured heart. I could not change what had happened, no matter how hard I cried and how petulant I became. Instead I simply had to accept it as best I could.

Gradually I found myself becoming more able to look back and see God's hand at work in the run-up to Richard's death. We had just enjoyed a lovely holiday with all of his family in Gloucestershire, and during that time had formed special friendships. Richard had finally reached a point where he was physically well after a long period of abdominal pain, and had been enjoying sport again even as he had immersed himself in his new job. I was grateful too that there were no outstanding issues between us as a couple. We had exchanged a few harsh words the night before he died, when work had eroded the time I had hoped we would spend together, but we had resolved our difficulties and were at peace.

Even in the details of his death, I could sense God's provision. Richard's suffering had seemed small, and I was so grateful that I had awoken in time and that the children had not been prematurely disturbed.

I now remembered conversations with Richard about what might happen if either of us died. He had repeatedly reassured me that life would go on, and had indeed preached about it shortly before he died, clearly saying that he believed that we would retain our hope. This memory bolstered my weakened faith, and gave me a new sense of determination. I did not want to let him or God down by admitting defeat and allowing the pernicious weeds of self-pity, jealousy, bitterness and despair to set seed and take root once again. I became almost feisty as I took up the challenge to fulfil Richard's words, and allow my faith to blossom and grow.

Gradually I was beginning to see some semblance of light on the horizon, however dim and distant. I saw that God did not want my heart to be full of anger and fear. The bitterness, the jealousy, the self-pity and despair were things that I had allowed and had not come from him. I had to start believing his words, and allow my hope to be found in him.

I clung to the promises he seemed to imprint on my mind, in particular one from Isaiah that had come the week after Richard's death. It was Isaiah 40:31:

> Those who hope in the LORD
>   will renew their strength.
> They will soar on wings like eagles;
>   they will run and not grow weary,
>   they will walk and not be faint.

I longed for the time when I would be able to fly again, and when my strength would return. And I recognized more surely than before that I would live to see that day. I knew it would be a long time until I could feel it in my heart, but the verse gave me strength to carry on through the heartache and pain.

Psalm 40:1 seemed to sum up how I felt: 'I waited patiently for the LORD; he turned to me and heard my cry.' I felt I had been hammering on God's chest, begging him for some pain relief. And I knew he had turned to me and heard my lament.

5 The snare of loneliness

As I continued to battle through the still intense darkness, I was aware that some major decisions were looming. I sorely missed the intimacy and companionship I had shared with Richard, and was desperate to experience deeper sharing once again.

Most days seemed to crawl past with barely a snippet of adult conversation, often snatched as I made my way from place to place. I was particularly aware of the sting of being alone as the new school term had commenced, and other parents arrived in the playground holding hands. Saying goodbye to my daughter as she began school was hard as I acknowledged the emptiness I felt within. It seemed that this fresh loss, albeit only part-time, merely served to heighten my inner barrenness, a barrenness that I knew the children would never be able to fill.

I yearned for human arms to surround me, and I wanted to be with someone who was truly mine. The intensity of my longings surprised me, as I did not yet feel ready to move on. I wanted Richard at my side, and in many ways continued to act as if I was married to him. The memories of our shared life were still fresh, and I felt as if I needed to unpick our marriage as I strove to move on. I was desperate to get this grief work done, especially now that I could see a dim and distant light to edge towards.

I found myself reliving the times I had shared with Richard, going steadily backwards in time. I remembered special family days, exploring new areas of countryside and looking for signs of wildlife. And I thought back to the rambles, even with a pushchair, and our often thwarted attempts at bird watching. But along with recollections of our happy moments and our joys, my mind was filled with memories that were less pleasant to replay, as I looked back on the times when I had failed Richard as a spouse by being less than the person I could have been. I recalled the conversations we had shared about trusting God, and how he had found it so difficult when I had seemed to go the other way. And I remembered the times I had hurt him by not sharing my inner conflicts and pain. I felt angry with myself for not being more understanding as he had struggled through the demands of a new job, and I was ashamed that I had nagged him so frequently to take more family time.

I could see now that the patterns I had adopted within the marriage, especially since the arrival of children, had sought to strangle his love, rather than help him to grow. I felt I had let him down in so many ways, and the pain was excruciatingly hard. I longed for a chance to make amends, to be a better wife, knowing what I now knew about myself. 'If only' was a constant refrain on my lips as I limped along.

Looking at Richard's pictures challenged me too, as I realized how much I still desired to be with him as man and wife. My body longed for the closeness that we had once shared, and I physically ached as I acknowledged that my still-active passion for him could never be assuaged.

The pain would come in waves, leaving me feeling wretched and ashamed. How could I look anyone else in the eye when I was still consumed with desire for Richard, and yet how could I resign myself to a life of celibacy after experiencing such intimacy and joy? The sobs would rack my body, leaving me gasping for breath and literally counting the minutes until they were gone.

Such was my feeling of shame that I felt unable to share this anguish with anyone. I felt dirty for having such lustful desires and suddenly became acutely aware of any single men around, seeing them as threats to my sanity and peace. I struggled to maintain eye contact when talking to males of any sort, and recoiled when male members of the wider family gave me a hug, worrying that if I relaxed into their embrace I would be undone. I longed for Richard and Richard alone, and yet I knew it could never be.

While alone in bed at night, feeling the cold emptiness at my side, the pain was particularly strong. I would sob uncontrollably into my pillow, longing for some respite from the sheer desolation of unrequited love. Torrents would sweep over me unasked for and unbidden, pain of such intense loneliness and aloneness that nothing and no-one could relieve.

And during the day too the pain would ambush me at times. Seeing an elderly couple walking along hand in hand would be enough to generate fresh pangs of loss, as I faced the fact that I was walking into the future alone. Knowing that God was by my side did not seem to be enough, and yet I could not face the thought of another man taking Richard's place.

I felt vulnerable and bare as the sides of me that had once been blended with Richard were now forcefully exposed. Increasingly I found it difficult to be around married friends, and yet I appreciated the chance to see the joy that partnership could bring, and the balanced male and female company it provided for us all. I was aware that my life was female-dominated these days, as I moved from one group of mums to another, and I so sorely missed interacting with males.

I also began to notice a new pattern emerging, one that directly correlated with my monthly cycles. How I hated what those hormones could do! I did as I had done so many times before, distracting myself with activity until the storm would pass each month, pushing my feelings to one side until I was alone. Then I could vent my frustration on God. I knew that he would understand. Daily I surrendered my longings for a partner to him, knowing that my life was in his hands. He alone was my Saviour, having died on the cross for me, and more than anything, I was desperate for more intimacy with him.

I found that the part of me that yearned so desperately to be with Richard was the same part that could say, 'I love you, Lord.' It seemed as if my love for Richard had been inextricably bound up with my love for God. Through knowing Richard I had glimpsed more of God's love and grace towards me, and I had come to understand more about what God was really like. I so needed to remember that reality when the loneliness would ensnare me once again, and to run into God's arms until the squall had passed.

And yet another major wrench was going on outside of me even as I was dealing with this turmoil within. A message came through that the diocese was appointing a replacement for Richard, and therefore our house might be required.

What would happen to us if they asked us to leave? I was petrified. In all the emotional upheaval of the last few months I had given scant thought to the practical business of moving on. We had been in this town for just over a year when Richard had died, and although we had made some good friendships, it did not feel like home. I longed to return to the town of my youth, where we had begun our married life, but was forced to accept that this would not be right for me just now. The friendship circle we had once enjoyed there had largely broken up as people had moved on, and the thought of starting all over again in my new circumstances filled me with dread. The sensible option was to stay put; at least here I was known, and people were willing to help.

Another option was the Derbyshire house, which Richard and I had bought some years ago as a retreat from vicarage life. It was a house that we had both loved, and into which we had poured much time and energy, making it a place where we could relax and unwind. The problem was that we had never lived there and therefore we knew very few people close by. To move there now would be utter folly and an open invitation to yet more isolation and loneliness. Reluctantly I came to the conclusion that it had to go.

I was grateful that my ties with the place had already been loosened a little as latterly it had been rented out. But when the tenant showed little inclination to leave and attempted to extract money from me for unauthorized improvements he had made, my heart sank. I struggled again with a deep sense of injustice that I should have to deal with all this hassle alone.

Eventually a stiffly worded legal letter saw him on his way, and I was able to move on. But going up there after he had left was one of the hardest 'firsts', and one I felt completely unable to face without the support of friends. Images of Richard haunted me everywhere I turned, as I came to terms with the scars on the furniture and the mess left behind. This house epitomized my shared life with Richard, and everything within it had some story attached.

I found myself wandering through the rooms and garden longing for just one more chance to love and care for this place, even as I prepared to clear it out. Friends hired a van to remove the furniture, and they brought others along to lend a hand. Yet more friends dug up plants from the garden that Richard and I had created together just before our daughter was born.

The whole house looked so barren and forlorn as I entrusted it to the agents for sale. I watched in frustration as winter approached and the initial flurry of viewings came to nothing. I felt shackled to it now, but knew that selling it was a key to me moving on.

Living in the vicarage was feeling increasingly uncomfortable, knowing that it had been promised elsewhere, and although the diocese had never once asked me to leave, I was anxious to go. Slowly the weeks ticked by with no glimmer of hope, while I threw myself into my routines, and tried not to think too far ahead. Daily I implored God to do the seemingly impossible and sell the house, and daily I struggled as no news came.

It was early autumn when the licensing for the new minister came around, and still the diocese did not ask me to leave. As she took her vows, I could barely bring myself to watch. These were the same words that Richard had spoken when we had first come to this place. Once again a wave of grief and loneliness threatened to throw me overboard.

I was racked by anxiety on behalf of the children, as I looked bleary-eyed into the future. Their sleep was getting increasingly disturbed, and often they seemed to wake up in the night sobbing for their daddy. How could I continue to cope with these two precious bundles on my own? Was this pain ever going to end? I knew I was not really searching for answers; I was simply allowing myself to grieve. But then a new question began to well up inside, one that the children articulated for me: what would become of them if I too were to die? The thought of a double abandonment was too painful for words.

My relief was enormous when Richard's brother and his wife agreed to support me in this new way. God was providing for me. And so my peace of mind returned, as I remembered that the burden of caring for my children was not one that I carried alone. God was there beside me each and every step of the way. He alone knew what the future would bring, and I could trust him for their care because above all they were his. Again I crawled back to God to ask for his forgiveness for my lack of trust in him, and to ask him to make me clean.

Knowing that God was with me in my parenting, however, did not suddenly produce an extra pair of hands. I now appreciated all the more what Richard and I had enjoyed together – the silly jokes, the understanding hugs, the encouraging comments, and the deep love for each other, for our offspring and for God. And I missed his help, especially with the children. They didn't always want to learn to take turns or wait for my attention, and as the emotional temperature increased, inevitably some or all of us would end up in tears. We would often finish by having team hugs at these moments, the children jostling with each other until I worked out what action needed to happen first. About that time I coined the phrase 'I'm not an octopus!' as an attempt to defuse the situation in a light-hearted way, and to help the children to recognize that I could not do everything at once.

There were times, too, when I had no choice but to ignore the demands of the outside world. It was not always physically possible to hold two children and answer the telephone or the doorbell at exactly the same time, and sometimes the children needed to know that I was there just for them. I wanted to let them know they were the most important people in my life now, and this seemed like a good place to start. I needed to carve out times when we could be fully present together and get used to being a family of three, and so I chose to let the answerphone pick up calls at mealtimes and bedtimes, as a way of showing my intentions to the children in a tangible form.

But it was hard not to be dragged down by the relentlessness of being alone. I had to remind myself that there had been many instances in any case when I had struggled on my own with the children, even when Richard had been alive. Mothering pre-schoolers was a draining and demanding job, despite the rewards, and I had to learn not to be too harsh on myself. And yet learning to accept that all I could do was my best, and that I was only able to do one thing at once, no matter how hard I tried, was not something that came easily to me.

Being 'only one pair of hands' had so many implications for family life. The activities that required a one-adult-to-one-child ratio could not be attempted without additional support. Even simple day excursions often felt too lonesome alone, and although in the early days my desire for company had been driven largely by practical concerns, I could now see that having others at my side was a way of alleviating the loneliness I often felt.

That loneliness plagued me on holidays too, as we left behind the support and security of the familiar. The only holidays that felt manageable were those shared with family and friends, but my restricted stamina and energy limited my horizons, and I could not face driving for more than an hour at a time without a stopover. Even as my energy had increased, the idea of holidaying alone had remained utterly terrifying, as I thought of the potential isolation and the gargantuan solo effort it would involve. Knowing that we would return to an empty house was an additional pain, and I would often feel a fresh pang of grief as I unlocked the door. No-one had missed us while we'd been gone, and no-one eagerly awaited our safe return. And unpacking the car while simultaneously entertaining children was a nightmare I could happily live without. Often I would catch myself wondering if the holiday had been worthwhile, providing any benefit at all to me, as I scrabbled to get everything sorted and put away.

But it wasn't just the practical aspects that allowed the loneliness and isolation to creep back in. Emotionally I would often return from holiday a complete wreck, having shelved all my turbulent feelings until I was back in the safety of my own home. There at least I could let them go, but I hated the post-holiday blues that seemed to descend on me as soon as we reached the front door. Returning and being suddenly wrenched away from those with whom we had just shared our time and confidences brought back the sharp sting of loneliness with a vengeance. Knowing that there was no-one with whom to share our holiday reminiscences and souvenirs simply added to the pain.

Readjusting to being on our own again often brought us all to tears as we grieved for those we had left behind. And as the children struggled to readapt to the limitations of my solo parenting, I would find myself once more longing for another pair of hands. In some small way these post-holiday difficulties were mirroring the greater picture of my grief. Getting used to being on my own was taking much longer than I had hoped, and my singleness was causing me much pain. All I could do was to race back to God and pour out my heart, and depend on him for my future once again.

6 Companions on the way

It was autumn 2005, and the pain had finally subsided into a constant dull throb. I had got through the summer intact, relieved that no more major disasters had occurred, and my daughter had started school. I was exhausted from the strain and emotional turmoil of life, and I longed for a rest. So much seemed unsettled, as groups we had belonged to for some time ceased to be part of our lives any more, and we did not know where we would be living and worshipping long term. A feeling of restlessness seemed to pervade everything I did as I strove to move forward into the future while still feeling increasingly tied to the past.

The house in Derbyshire remained unsold, and began to feel like a millstone around my neck. Indeed, it felt as if the whole issue of our future housing rested on that sale, and I found myself begging God time and again to get it sold. My confidence began to waver as I considered changing tack, and I wondered to whom I should turn.

Asking for help in any shape or form was something I had been struggling with for some time. I felt so bruised and battered by my turbulent emotions that my reserves seemed almost gone. I could not face the thought of being rejected if a request for help was refused, or picking up the pieces if a job was left only half done, so it seemed preferable therefore to try to soldier on alone. I did not want to admit how weak and inadequate I was feeling as I tried to keep so many balls up in the air. Surely I should be strong enough to cope on my own now that I was in the second year of my grief.

In the initial days of my bereavement, when I had been totally overwhelmed, I had found it easier to accept the many offers of help that I had received. The church had been at the forefront, providing countless meals and helping in many other practical ways, while both sides of the family had done their best to ease the strain. Local friends too had helped me to cope, and those from further afield had kept me constantly in their thoughts and prayers. I had greatly appreciated all the assistance I had been given. But as time had worn on and offers had gradually dried up, I had felt increasingly awkward about finding the courage to ask for assistance. It felt like a delicate balancing act, knowing whom to ask and for what, and how often it was reasonable to request support.

The notion of imposing my demands on others was abhorrent to me, and I could not bear the thought of becoming someone who made people's hearts sink. Nor did I want to interfere with their time to relax, as I knew from experience how precious that was. And so I often left things as long as I dared, desperately hoping that someone would offer before I had to stick out my neck and ask.

If the practical things were difficult to ask for, then seeking emotional support was downright impossible most of the time. I didn't want to encumber others with my pain, especially as time went on, and I felt I should be able to cope on my own. I found it tricky explaining my chaotic emotions and the intensity of my loneliness to those who had never endured such grief. I felt raw and exposed when I said I was struggling, and the cost just felt too great.

Instead I poured my limited energy into keeping the lid on my pain, and avoiding showing it to the world. I became adept at sidestepping questions meant as pleasantries and deflecting answers on to more superficial levels, in an attempt to protect myself. I had always been one for just a few good friends, and these were the ones I gathered around myself now, as if to shield myself from the world. These were the ones who had become precious to me as I had waded through the first torrid year of grief, and I knew I needed to share my feelings of unrest with them.

But despite this, I still found it hard to share my emotions much of the time. I did not think that others would be interested in my petty woes, and was aware that my feelings changed significantly from day to day. Nor did I want to worry those closest to me when my mood dipped and I felt full of despair. Those who were less close to me could definitely not be told, for then they might ply me with pity or treat me as just another pastoral case. The conclusion I therefore came to was that I could seldom appear to be in need. As a result, I was becoming more and more independent as time went on, almost fiercely so, gradually distancing myself from those who cared.

In late October a viewing was finally arranged for the Derbyshire house, and a low offer was received. I agonized over whether or not to accept it, as the asking price had already been substantially reduced, and I wasn't sure if my faith would rise to the challenge of trusting God to make the sums work when it came to buying somewhere new. As if in answer, I had a phone call to say the offer had been increased. It wasn't by much, but it was the confirmation I required: God was in this and I had to learn to trust him. But as the days went by without any sign of progress, my faith faltered and I began to wonder if I would soon be back to square one. I was finding it so hard to exercise my still-feeble trust in God, even though I knew I had no real option but to leave it with him.

As always, I threw myself into the groups we were part of, seeing them as a distraction from pain. I knew I was immensely tired, but my restlessness meant that I found it hard to sit still. At least when I was occupied, the mental whirring lessened for a while, and I could use the time profitably to benefit others as well as myself. I had always enjoyed giving in a practical way, and so I found myself offering to help with the toddler groups we attended. It felt good to be able to give again rather than always being on the receiving end, and I was grateful that my physical stamina was holding out. Emotionally, however, my strength was quite limited, as I still felt so fractured within. And yet so often I seemed to find myself taking other people's problems on board, eager to support them in their plight, in order to distract myself from my own. I did not want to accept that I was not ready for this just now and that I was expecting too much of myself.

The upside, however, was that I was starting to make new friends. I was all too well aware that, through no fault of their own, many people had been unable to accompany me on my long journey through grief. Some had slipped quietly away as time had gone on, facing new challenges of their own. Others had felt the pain too keenly themselves to comfort me. I knew that my inner circle of solid friends would continue to be extremely important to me, but I also knew that I did not want to be totally dependent on them. And so I was thrilled when my offers to help at groups produced seeds of friendship that looked promising and good. These were the excuse I gave myself to continue to give out and be useful once again. But the downside was that I felt in need of more time on my own to recuperate.

My son had now begun pre-school part-time, but it seemed from his uncharacteristically withdrawn behaviour that I had made a bad choice. My eagerness to give closure in one area at least had meant a hasty decision that I had not discussed with anyone else. I felt foolish that I had acted in this way, and needed to admit my mistake, while looking for an alternative that would suit him better and fit geographically when we finally managed to move house.

The school I had chosen was quite near the centre of the town. Finding a playgroup nearby where my son would meet others who would go to that school seemed to be the sensible option. This time I asked around, anxious not to repeat my error. It was not long before a replacement pre-school was found, one where my son could spend his boundless energy and thrive. Yet another piece of the jigsaw puzzle of our future seemed to be fitting into place.

But the little steps of outward progress did little to assuage the immense impatience I was feeling inside. I had been fortunate in finding an excellent Christian counsellor shortly after Richard's death, and the sessions I shared with her had become a safe haven as I had battled through my storms. Now I needed to be more honest and go deeper into my pain, expressing my immense frustration at the lack of movement in my life, and allowing myself to feel the hurt that I had bottled up inside. I knew that I needed to forgive those who had unwittingly caused me pain by their thoughtless comments and failure to show concern. And I knew too that I needed to accept some of the blame. But I did not feel ready to let go of my pain. I still wanted to cling to the agony of grief that made up such a huge part of my identity, and use it to justify keeping others at arm's length.

To me it was obvious they had not behaved as they should have done, and that they were clearly in the wrong. They ought to have known what I needed without me having to ask all the time, and I felt justified in feeling isolated and alone. Yet I knew if I stopped to think about it that many had in fact been ready to walk with me through my grief. Indeed, many had shown their willingness to do anything and everything they could to help me on my way. I did not want to face the fact that it was my churlishness and arrogance that had slowly pushed them aside.

Church was still an enormous source of pain, and yet I could not tear myself away. The help and practical support I had received from friends there had been so great, but despite this, I felt completely unable to share my inner torment, something that was grating with me more and more.

As I spoke to trusted friends, I began to see that it was increasingly hard for me to worship God in a place that was so full of anguish for me. Another decision had to be made. It took an outsider to shake me from my complacency. He expressed his surprise that I still remained there, yet I hated being disloyal to Richard by moving on. I did not want to upset the children by tearing them away from their spiritual home, and I did not want to upset those who had cared for me for so long. To leave would be to remove the one remaining link in our weekly routine that had been unchanged since before Richard had died. And I knew that by going I would be cutting all ties with this place. But friends had also pointed out, and I had sensed it for myself, that I could not bring up my children to know and love God if I myself was spiritually dead inside. I knew that I had to look after myself spiritually if I was to look after them.

Even so, I found it hard to say goodbye to a place that was so redolent with memories of Richard, a place that was the sole reason why we had come to this town. I grieved for the future I would never have in this place, and longed for it to be made whole even as I prayed for healing for myself.

As December began, I knew that this Christmas would be our last one at the church. I was not sure exactly when we would go, but the internal decision had been made. We would have to find a new church. Slowly I began to cut my ties, knowing I was still very sensitive to losses of any kind.

It seemed strangely significant coming to the eighteen-month anniversary of Richard's death as Christmas approached, and I felt an odd sense of achievement at having survived. I knew that there were many changes ahead, and still much inner work to be done, but slowly I was beginning to look forward to the chance to make a fresh start.

Within a few days the house sale was suddenly completed, as if in response to my new-found hope, and Christmas came. The pangs of loneliness clawed at my heart once more, but resolutely I pushed on, hoping that the New Year would bring more joy.

I could see now, as I looked back, just how many people had been supporting me. Even in the depths of my despair, when I had felt so desperately alone, God had been providing and showing me that he cared. My family and the wider Fair family had visited and telephoned me regularly and had constantly upheld me in their prayers. And my inner ring of close friends had given me ample time and space to share my anguish, while pointing me to the only one who could heal my pain. There were many others, both locally and further afield, who had ministered to me in a multitude of different ways, and I knew that God had been working through them too. It was astonishing to me now how I had overlooked all this support. I had been so busy living in the story of my widowhood and pain that I had failed to see the companionship still available.

I realized that I had become almost phobic about allowing myself to depend on others in any way, and my justification of not bothering them was wearing a little thin. Of course they had families and needs of their own, but if they had expressed a desire to assist me in some way, then I had to learn to take them at their word. By depriving them of the opportunity to give, I was denying them the chance to use their gifts, and even blocking an avenue for God to work in.

Gradually I saw that my new-found independence was actually strangling my desire for companionship. I had become intoxicated by its power, as it had liberated me from the dependency I had struggled with for so long. Increasingly I was becoming disenchanted with its heady perfume, and yet I felt trapped into continuing, as I could see no other way. God was calling me to something more, but I was still so frightened of letting others into my life and showing them my pain.

It was a sermon that finally gave me the answer I was looking for. As I listened, I discovered that God's way was neither dependence nor independence. Rather it was a different way of being, that of inter-dependence, a type of relationship in which I was called to live in community with other people, sharing my joys and sorrows in a mutually reciprocating way, and co-existing as equals in God's sight. It was in this context that God wanted me to grow.

He did not want me to continue to nurse my bruises, or even to bring them solely to him. Rather he wanted me to begin to explain the turmoil within and be vulnerable enough to share my struggles with those who cared. I needed to learn to accept his love through the many companions he had given me and allow them to be the physical expressions of his care. And I needed to allow others to contribute to my life and support me, even as they allowed me to do the same for them.

Once again I found myself on my knees, asking for God's forgiveness for my sin. My fierce independence and stubborn pride had cost me many tears alone as I had pushed both other people and God away. It was only with God's help that I would be able to open up and share my innermost pain.

7 Recovering a sense of self

New Year dawned bright and clear, but with it came an unexpected slump in my mood. The aftermath of the unanticipated euphoria at the sudden sale of the Derbyshire house after months of frustration and despair, combined with the stamina required to get through Christmas alone, resulted in me being thrust once again into sharp and searing pain. Everyone about me seemed to be looking forward to the year ahead, enjoying family fun as the holiday season came to an end, while I would crawl through each day, often ending up in a pool of tears.

The future seemed like a dark, gaping chasm full of unknowns, and the path to get there was strewn with yet more losses as links to the past were progressively being torn away. I found myself looking ahead with trepidation and fear as I contemplated the changes the year ahead would bring for us all. I longed for some mental space away from the children to try to process my grief, and yet I also feared time alone, worrying that if I let myself go I might never regain my composure. The shock waves of Richard's death were still reverberating in an all-too-forceful way, and I was struggling to know who I was underneath the rubble that was left.

As the new school term began, there were fresh challenges. My son was starting his new playgroup, and therefore I would be making new contacts and building new routines. We had said goodbye to the toddler group at church, a fixture that had been part of our lives for almost three years, and the feelings of loss were profound.

I felt as if I had been through so much over the last nineteen months as I had come to terms with the consequences of Richard's death, and it seemed that there were precious few traces left of the normality of the life that I had once known and loved. So many areas of life felt uncertain, especially regarding church and home, and I was desperate to press on and get it all sorted as fast as possible so that our lives could settle down and once more become stable and secure.

Inside a great untangling was going on, as I sought to separate out what had related to the partnership that had been Richard-and-Janine, and what was purely and simply Janine. I needed to extricate myself from the tangled mess of the past and all I had invested in the future I had hoped to share with Richard, and work out what I wanted to carry forward for myself. The sorting and sifting of Richard's possessions was something I had been trying to tackle for some time. Even in the first few weeks of grief I had been able to let go of some of his things. His clothes had seemed to taunt me, hanging unused in his wardrobe space, and therefore many of them had been dispatched to a shelter for homeless men. Finding outlets where his possessions would be put to good use was important to me, even as I had fought my way through the freshness of the pain.

There were a few key items that I had been unable to relinquish, like the pyjamas he had been wearing when he died. They had been swiftly washed and ironed within the first week, even though they were badly torn from the resuscitation attempt, but that had not felt enough. Finally

I plucked up the courage to ask someone to mend them for me as best they could, a symbolic act that I felt was a necessary marker of my own movement forward, and I think also meaningful to the person who patched and mended them. There were one or two items that I wanted to offer to others, things that I hoped would be useful to them, as well as giving the items a new lease of life. And the children had requested Richard's big blue wind-stopper jumper to snuggle up with, so that was kept back too, along with a pullover of which I was particularly fond.

The biggest area to tackle, however, was the issue of Richard's study, a room full of memories and grief. Ever since we had first looked around the house and seen its size, this room had been a source of pain to me. Because of the layout of the house it was never going to be possible to make it the main living room, especially while the children were so young. But I had been determined to make it a more useful area and had spent many hours in there alone when the children were asleep, trying to make the agony less severe. Bags of items that I had sorted and felt ready to release were stored in there, awaiting new homes, and as the Derbyshire house had been sold, much of the excess furniture had come to reside in the remaining space. It was a room that would always be full of associations with Richard, but at least I could now face bringing the children in from time to time without it always reducing me to tears.

Sorting out the vast quantities of paperwork from Richard's job had been an enormous task through which I had attempted to wade. I had read hundreds of emails to ascertain what I needed to keep. I had emptied and cleared the desk also, to make way for the new files I had to create as I dealt with the financial and legal implications of Richard's death. And the extensive book collection Richard had built up had to be whittled down. Offering clergy friends the chance to take what they wanted for their own use made the loss more manageable, knowing that the books and resources would be in good hands.

But Richard's clerical attire was more difficult to release, not least because his shirts had been especially made to fit his pencil-thin neck. I wasn't sure I could face seeing others in the brightly coloured shirts he had worn with such enthusiasm, and so I finally sent them off to his old theological college some distance away, in the hope that they might find a home with some impoverished ordinand, free from memories of the past.

Another painful area was the outhouse and shed. Richard had built up an extensive collection of wood and woodworking tools, and I needed to find homes where they would be loved and well used.

But it wasn't simply Richard's own possessions that had to be reviewed. Within the first month of Richard's death I realized I would need to make a decision regarding cars. I could not justify having two on the drive. The big estate car felt too awkward and inefficient for the amount of driving I did about town, while the old runabout I had used for work was too small and unreliable for our family needs. Thankfully my parents graciously stepped in and offered to help. I borrowed a friend's husband to help me with the negotiations, and landed my first major deal, trading in the estate car for a new one that was medium-sized and suited us down to the ground. Giving the other one away to a friend was a happy by-product that made me smile.

It was not just the car, though, that had to be downsized. I was very aware that any house I could afford to buy would be substantially smaller than the vicarage I was now in, and I would therefore need to be rather radical in the task of slimming down as I attempted to condense two houses into one. I had also been given some items from John's flat, and consequently my vicarage house seemed to be overflowing with excess furniture. The problem was that I had no idea where we were going to live. Trying to work out what would fit and what would not was impossible without that detailed knowledge. All I could do was try to assess what I definitely did not want to carry forward, and what I might possibly want to keep if space allowed.

It was gruelling sorting out what was important to me and what I wanted to bring forward into my new life alone. I knew I needed to get rid of the things that would hold me back and drag me down, and I realized that I needed to make changes in our present house as a symbol of this. I began to remove the pictures that made me feel sad, and put up new pictures and hanging toys to brighten the walls. I stuck the cards I received, and the promises I felt God was speaking into my life, in prominent places to encourage me as I went about my chores, and bought flowers for myself, just as Richard had done many times in the past, to distract me from my pain.

Several rooms began to take on a different feel as furniture was swapped around and items disappeared for good. The old sofa Richard had bought before we were married was quickly dispatched to make way for the far more comfortable Derbyshire ones, and the sideboard I had never really liked was given away. Kitchen equipment was reshuffled and the extras given to those setting up new homes, and the large table Richard had commissioned was donated to close friends.

It seemed that there was always something I was wanting to give away to some poor unsuspecting visitor, and it became a bit of a joke that no-one could leave the house empty-handed or without agreeing to come back and collect something later on.

And yet despite the sorting and my protestations about wanting to move on, I found myself reluctant to embrace the change. The searing pain left me feeling too vulnerable and raw to grasp hold of what needed to be done, except on a very superficial level, and although I was slowly learning to ask for help, I could not face admitting to the unstable emotions that seemed to cloud my days. The tussle to let go of the joint past with Richard was draining me of my scanty emotional reserves, and it did not take much to leave me feeling wounded and hurt. I felt as if I were pushing an immensely heavy load uphill.

My excuses for staying in the vicarage were running out now that the Derbyshire house had been sold, and so I tried to throw myself into the task of house hunting. The diocese offered to help me, and I knew that this was well meant, but a part of me resented it as I still did not feel ready to leave.

Alongside this I continued to agonize over my decision to leave the church. Somehow being surrounded by those memories of Richard each and every time I went in was both comforting and disturbing. They allowed me to feel some connection with him even after all this time, and provided some security as the rest of my life continued to change shape. But they also produced such intense pangs of stabbing pain that worshipping God was almost impossible at times. What I had known in my head for a while about the need to move on to new spiritual pastures was finally beginning to sink down to my heart.

I had to face up to the fact that the future was for me to navigate alone. And I had to begin to move towards the horizon in a way that was right for me as an individual, not as a component of an equation that was Richard-and-Janine. An important element of that letting go had to include the church which was bound up with my identity as part of a clergy couple, and, as difficult as I found it to explain to others, that meant we had to leave. Asking for prayers from those who had been supporting me in the church felt like a gigantic first step to take, and one I bottled out of many times. But God was gracious, and the opportunities to speak up came around again and again until I was ready to accept the invitation he gave. Yet even then I could only hint at what was ahead, preferring to admit to feeling unsettled rather than draw a definitive line under this chapter of my life.

It seemed far more appealing simply to walk away from the church without telling anyone, and leave them to work it out for themselves. I knew that many would misunderstand my reasons for leaving, and as yet I felt too fragile to explain it, except to those whom I knew would take it well. They had seen the signs of my unrest for some time, and already knew what I had been so slow to accept, that I had to move on in order to be more fully myself. They were the ones who encouraged me, and picked up the pieces when I found myself absorbing fresh new waves of pain as I told those who were less able to react in a positive way. Slowly I was facing up to the inevitable and allowing myself to loosen the remaining ties to the past and the church.

The links with a new parish had already started to form through a parents-and-toddlers' group I had begun to attend there. As the spring term started and I was asked to help run the group, I took this as a sign that I was on the right track, and now felt more able to share my journey of transition with a wider circle. I was encouraged by the value my new-found friends were placing on me and the interest they showed, and this helped to soften the blow.

The next step was to start attending occasional services at the new church to make sure it was somewhere I could feel spiritually at home. But it felt so odd driving into town on that first Sunday elsewhere. Although we had been there once in the past with Richard on one of his rare Sundays off, it still felt like foreign ground.

Once again the pain took me by surprise. I had steeled myself for the inevitable questions, and for the emotional energy required to make new contacts and friends, but I had not anticipated the pain of seeing someone else in clerical robes at the front of a church, and finding myself wishing it was Richard. It was all too easy to think how he would have led the worship, and the confidence with which he would have greeted the unexpected happenings that went on. I felt completely ambushed by the pain of my memories of him as I strove desperately to stay in control and make a good start. I longed to feel at home in that church, and begin to grow again, and I resented the fact that the pain had followed me there. But I knew I needed to press on and make new connections, both for myself and for the children's sakes. They needed new friends to replace the ones they had lost, and I knew that I just had to give it time. Attending once a month wasn't an ideal way to begin, but it was all I could cope with at this stage, as my battered heart felt the strain. At least I was assured of a few friendly faces around, both from the toddler group and from a close friend who was now part of the clergy team. The hard part was that, as I changed churches, I would need to stop seeing the counsellor who had walked with me for so long through the darkest depths of my pain.

It was Mothering Sunday when I finally made the break with the church that had held me for so long. It had been just over three years since Richard had been licensed to minister there. How shockingly different and unexpected were my circumstances now. It seemed inappropriate to make a fuss. Now I was simply another parishioner deserting the ranks, and, much as I longed for some public affirmation of the role I had played at Richard's side, it felt too painful to look for that now. What had begun so promisingly with Richard all those years ago had fizzled to nothing, and I was leaving, feeling ashamed that my grief had kept me from accepting God's blessings in this place.

The vicar respected my wishes to keep things quiet, and our departure was limited to a one-line mention in the prayers. I was stunned that it was over so fast. The children had been given little gifts in their Sunday groups, something that meant a great deal. But as I walked away for one last time, with the children in tow, back to the vicarage that was part of the past, I was barely able to contain my tears.

A strange sense of relief that the weeks of duplicity were over was intermingled with a scorching pain. My heart throbbed in agony as I severed the last tie with the church that had played such a central role in my life for so long. I wasn't sure if I would ever manage to face going back there again, so painful were the memories attached, but I knew deep down that I had done the right thing in moving on.

Sundays now took on a different pattern as we went to the new church in town week by week. It felt like an act of faith simply driving across town to get there as we waited for a new house to appear. One day I hoped we would be able to walk to church from our own home nearby, but for now all I could do was wait and trust in God to provide in the time and the way that he saw fit.

As we made our way through the services each week, I was conscious of feeling very exposed. I was making a new start on my own as a widow, without being able to hide behind my role as Richard's wife or a clergy spouse. It felt so long since I had been an ordinary parishioner in a church, or even been to a different church on my own without some connection to Richard being made. I wanted to be able to talk about him still as I forged on into the future, and felt pangs of sadness that many of the people I was now mixing with had never known him. Keeping his memory alive was important to me, both for my sake and the children's, and yet being with people who barely knew me meant that this was increasingly hard.

I wanted to be able to celebrate what I had shared with Richard, not hide it away in a cupboard and be too embarrassed to mention his name. He had helped to shape me into the person I was now, and although our paths had diverged significantly when he had died, he was very much alive in my heart. As I spoke of him to those around, I was more able to see what had now become a part of myself. I found it easier to express who I was in these new surroundings where I was almost unknown, and to be more fully myself.

Looking back I realized that my style had been hampered by clinging on to the old church for so long, and that I had been crushing my own desire to grow. In my anxiety to show others there that I had not forgotten Richard or moved on too fast, I had allowed myself to cling to the past and use the old church as a scapegoat. Gaining some distance enabled me to see my own lack of progress in a clearer way, and I realized afresh that I still had a very long way to go. I could not rush along this path of grief, no matter how hard I tried, and I would have to let it unfold in its own time and way. The taste of hope I had experienced was luring me on, and I was keen to move on into the future fast. But accepting my impatience, and the frustrations I felt as making friendships took more time than I had hoped, was something that I found incredibly difficult.

The biggest question in my mind was when and specifically to where we would move. I began to trawl the estate agents with increasing urgency, anxious to find the right house, a home free from memories, especially those of Richard's death. I was fed up of the 'Saturday-morning-itis', as I termed it, when the light first streamed in at the window, and I found myself reliving the events of Richard's demise week after week.

In a vain attempt to assuage my restlessness, I tried to find new projects to pursue. I began to dig out old photographs and make little albums for the children with pictures of them with their daddy. These I placed in special memory boxes with some of his things that I had kept. It felt as though I was starting to be able to look back and give thanks for the positive memories, rather than just be engulfed by the pain. Of course the pain was still there, and still very real, but the bitter sting was easing slightly, and there were fleeting moments in each day when I would feel free from the heaviness I had felt for so long.

Slowly but surely a new self was starting to emerge from the rubble. With each decision I was making, I was learning again what I liked and disliked, what made me happy and what brought tears to my eyes. I began to dig deeper as I mentally separated myself from being part of the couple that had been Richard-and-Janine. It was exhausting dealing with the myriad choices that I had to make each day, and I would so long for something I didn't have to make a decision about. Yet it seemed that all of these decisions were making me face up to myself. For years I had tried to hide behind Richard and his preferences, convincing myself that he knew best. Now I had to do it all on my own. I was the one who decided if we left the house or stayed in, what car insurance to buy or which playgroup to use. I was the one who chose the food we bought and the clothes we wore. And I was the one who had decided where we would go to church. With each decision, I was gradually getting more in touch with myself.

In an attempt to push on further with this new work of getting to know myself, I decided to collect pictures to help me on my way. Amongst the cards I had kept from friends and well-wishers were those that held images with particular meaning for me: paintings of open doors or of flowers coming into full bloom, pictures of tapestries woven with richly coloured threads, dark colours mingling with brighter hues. And there was a photograph of a wild waterfall, cascading powerfully into a deep dark chasm, alongside a depiction of a quiet brook gently trickling along beside a stony path. I noticed images in magazines that I liked, and added those to my collection, along with sketches of jagged jigsaw pieces and of big hands holding an infant up as she wobbled on her way. And I searched out prints of open hands, a symbol of my willingness to allow God to use my grief as he chose. These images all spoke deeply to me in ways that words could not reach.

I started to store these pictures in a book so that I could come back to them whenever I needed to get in touch with myself again, to inspire me in my more forlorn moments and speak to me deep inside. I called it 'my little book of me', and filled it with pictures and cuttings that made me relax and smile, as well as reminding me of special times with God. It was a book that I could savour and enjoy when life was pulling me apart, and one which spoke to me of the bigger picture of my life. Gradually the self that had been buried under so much heaviness and weight was starting to emerge.

8 Forging a new identity

As we began to settle into the new church and make new friends, I was painfully aware that I still felt stuck regarding the house. The only thing I could focus on now was finding a suitable home, one that was right for the three of us and within my limited means, and I desperately hoped that when I found it the incessant ache within my heart would subside. I had done almost all I could of the general sorting and sifting, and was anxious to refine my endeavours by knowing the specifics of the house we would buy. My frustrations were mounting with having to use the car to get to the various weekly activities in town, including school and church, and I longed to find a place from which it would be possible to walk.

I was fed up trawling around the estate agents week after week with very little to show for my efforts, and felt exasperated when nothing new came up as I searched the internet day after day. Once again I found myself ranting and railing at God, impatient for him to act. I could not understand what all the delay was about. He knew more clearly than I did that I needed to move out of the old house, as much for my own sanity as for the benefit of the diocese, and he knew that I had done all I could to hurry things on their way.

But my ranting and railing only served to clear the air between us, and allow me to crawl back into God's arms, feeling foolish that once again I had been omitting to trust him. Ultimately I had to acknowledge that God knew what was best for me. I might not want this enforced period of waiting, and I might try to kick against it as much as I could, but he was in control; I had to let him be the one to provide. My striving and my struggling to make things happen was merely draining and exhausting me as I continued at my usual frantic pace, and yet I knew I had to do something to keep active so that I did not grind to a complete halt.

And so I continued to search, making list upon list of what I was looking for. The main criteria were easy to establish: a location near the town centre so that we could walk to our activities as much as possible, three bedrooms, a moderate garden, and a kitchen with room for us to dine in. Beyond that, the wish list was negotiable, although I knew it would be sensible to find somewhere that was easy to maintain. The problem was that the only houses coming on to the market were either too small or needed too much work doing for me even to consider looking around them. It was a gruelling time of waiting which tested my patience to the limit, and often found me in tears of desperation as I implored God to act.

The lessons in patience that I had been so slow to learn when the Derbyshire house was being sold were now being repeated, as if to reinforce the message that it was God's timing that was perfect and not my own. I clung to the promise I had been given some time earlier about God providing even the sparrows and swallows with a place to call home, words taken from a song of intense longing to dwell close to God's house (Psalm 84:3), and words that I now used to try to persuade God to alter his schedule. I jumped each time the phone rang, hoping that some news would come, and scoured the papers endlessly, searching for my perfect home. I was utterly worn out.

Finally a tiny picture in the local newspaper caught my eye. It showed a three-bedroomed property in the right location, and my hopes began to rise. Upon enquiring, the agent told me it had been on the market for a while, and so, nervously, I requested a viewing and enlisted the help of a friend to accompany me. The visit was scheduled for the end of the week, and I could hardly wait. I was a bag of nerves as I tried to carry on with the rest of life as normal and focus on the moment in hand. Looking around a house with an eye to buying it was a huge step forward, and I had severely underestimated how much emotional energy it would require. I steeled myself for potential disappointment and tried not to let my hopes soar too high.

Unexpectedly the viewing was brought forward by a day, and so I ended up going around the house alone, uncertain what I should be looking for objectively, and trying not to get too carried away with emotion as I began to love what I saw. It was a small house compared to where we were currently living, as I knew it would be, but it was quite new, and it looked like it would be manageable for me on my own. The location was all I could have asked for, and the stunning views over trees were a bonus I could never have imagined so near to the centre of town. It ticked all the necessary boxes on my wish list, and even some of the ones that were more desires than needs. Maybe this was the property that God had in mind? I was surprised I had not noticed it before, but perhaps I had not been ready to see it until now. There was one big snag however: it was a little over my budget.

Never being one to beat about the bush, I quickly explained my situation to the vendor and said I would be making an offer that day. My heart had fallen for the house hook, line and sinker, and I wanted it to be mine. It took two days for them to respond: the offer was declined. I was stunned. I felt as if I had been slapped in the face when I was barely recovering from the first blow. And it hurt. I battled with my disappointment, not sure how to proceed. I knew that I could not increase my offer, and hoped that the fact that I was a cash buyer and there was no chain attached would make the owners change their mind.

But the days went by and I heard nothing more. I was confused. Maybe I had got it all wrong, and this house was not the one. Maybe my heart had got carried away too fast and I had rushed in with the offer too soon. I did not want to play games with the vendors and string things out, but perhaps my honesty was being abused, and they were testing me to see if my resolve would weaken and the offer would increase. All I could do was crawl back to God and ask for his help to get through. I did not understand why I should have to go through the emotional turmoil of having my offer rejected. He knew the financial equations better than I did, and it felt grossly unfair. Again I found myself wailing at him and pouring out my anger, and again the only answer that I received to my unjust accusations of unfairness was that I could trust him. He would provide what was right for me, if I allowed him to, and he would give me the patience I needed to get through.

Reluctantly I began to look again. A week later I had another call from the agent to ask if I was still interested in the house. My hopes began to rise again, and yet I dared not believe that it was true. Could this be the signal I had been waiting for that the house would one day be mine? I decided to view it for a second time, with a friend, to reassure myself that I was doing the right thing. It was as lovely as I remembered it, and just as small. Again I repeated my offer, and waited to see how things would unfold. But now there was another cash buyer on the scene, and the wait was even more excruciating than the first one. A few days later the offer was again declined as the vendors' own negotiations on the house they wished to purchase fell through. Once again I was back to the start, wondering how I could keep going on this emotional roller coaster. I felt as if my patience were being stretched to new limits. Part of me still wanted to believe that the house would one day be mine, as I found myself comparing it unfavourably with other properties, and yet I desperately wanted to be able to put it out of my mind because I felt unwilling to deal with more rejection and pain. Perhaps God had something better for me that I was as yet unaware of, or perhaps there was some problem with this one that I had not found out?

All I knew was that God was bigger than any equation I could construct to get that house for myself, and it was no use striving to do things without him. He had promised to provide for me over and over again, and I was so slow to take him at his word. He wanted to give me somewhere that would be a blessing to us as a family of three, somewhere that would allow us to blossom and grow, and if I chose to do things without him then I would end up settling for less than the best. It was not a happy thought. I found myself asking God to take what little trust I did possess and to provide what else I needed to help me trust him more.

And so I continued to scour the papers and the internet, seeing nothing even vaguely similar. I looked around some older properties, each time hoping against hope that this would be better than the first and offer more potential than the paperwork seemed to imply, but each time it became apparent that the house simply would not do. The way my heart sank when I viewed each property showed me that I could never live there, and the amount of work required before we could even move in was always more than first met the eye. Faithful friends encouraged me as best they could as the hopefulness of spring seemed to leave me cold, and my moods swung up and down with the changing winds. I felt embarrassed that it was taking me so long to move out of the diocesan house, and dreaded contact with those in charge in case they should directly ask me to leave.

The pressure was eased somewhat when I learned via clergy friends that the diocese was in the process of buying another house. But this knowledge merely fuelled my impatience to move on. I did not want to keep living in the limbo land of uncertainty any more. The vicarage was increasingly feeling less like a home and more like a sorting office, and I longed for somewhere of my own in which I could relax. On one level I felt at the end of my tether, yet on another, I was strangely at peace. I knew that trusting God was the only way I could get through this restless period, and was slowly learning to pour out my frustrations to him.

Suddenly, just when I felt ready to give up completely and find a different tack, the agents phoned again. The vendor wanted to know if I was still interested. I couldn't believe my ears! My feet felt as though they were barely touching the floor. Quickly I arranged another viewing to reassure myself that my memory had not played tricks and painted everything with a rosy glow. Once again I reiterated the same offer I had made all those weeks ago. This time it was accepted without a fuss, and I was finally on my way. I could hardly contain my feelings of exhilaration.

Now I could complete all the sifting and sorting. I could plan specifically what would fit in each room, and give the rest away. I went around the new house again, measuring everything I could think of so that I could draw up detailed plans. The Derbyshire sofas looked too big for the new house, and so they were rehomed. Instead the high-backed one from John's flat could be pressed into action, and I looked forward to sinking into its comfy form. The children needed new beds to fit in their much smaller rooms, and a new smaller table had to be bought. We made endless trips to furniture warehouses as I tried to find the best buys. My priority was to make a new home where I felt relaxed and comfortable, a place in which I wanted to spend my time. I needed to surround myself with objects that would lift my spirits, rather than ones that made me feel sad, and I needed to incorporate as much joy as I could.

Many of the Derbyshire items fitted this description as they had been chosen with care and attention to detail, and so they were brought into service once again. It was amazing how they fitted so perfectly together to make a unified whole with the items from the vicarage. I was delighted by the way that objects I could no longer use turned out to be just what others were looking for, and almost ceased to be surprised when yet another possession that I needed to relinquish found its way into the hands of someone desperate for that very same piece. It was thrilling watching things take shape at long last, knowing that the months of waiting for my prayers to be answered were coming to an end. Now I could begin to look forward with anticipation and hope to a new beginning.

The long delays in the spring had allowed me gradually to peel myself away from our vicarage house emotionally. I was now more than ready to let it go and move on. A cross-stitch picture that I had finished some time earlier with the words 'Peace be in this house' emblazoned across it summed up what I felt. I wanted our new home to be a house of peace.

As I mentally started to move into the new house that would soon be ours, I began to feel much stronger in myself. This new place was just right for us as a family of three, and it felt like God's gift to us. Every time I looked at it when I drove past, my heart was filled with gratitude. I had professional photographs taken of our diminished family unit, to celebrate who we were now as a threesome. These would take a central place on the wall in the lounge. The photographs of the four of us that had been up in the old house were moved to a less prominent position, where I could choose to look at them if I wanted to, but didn't have to face them on the days when the pain felt too great. Those days still came with alarming regularity, when the magnitude of what I was about to do hit me with fresh vigour. Saying goodbye to the old life and buying a new house on my own was an enormous undertaking; just thinking about all that needed to be accomplished made me feel dizzy with fear. I had no idea how it would all come together in the end, or how we would physically move home. The sums of money involved in the purchase made me feel giddy, and I longed again for Richard's help and wisdom as I negotiated the transaction alone.

But at least there were days now when I could appreciate the warmth of the sunshine outside, and the sky did not always seem so grey. And the pain was not always foremost in my mind as I coped with the endless tasks that needed to be done. I busied myself in choosing light and airy colours for the walls, and made curtains and soft furnishings to complete the rooms. I passed on the toys the children had outgrown and downsized what was left. I emptied the vicarage loft of the boxes that had been stored up there, and sorted out what remained in the garage. And I potted up plants from the garden to take along. I packed the remaining boxes in eager anticipation, throwing myself into the process with as much energy as I could muster, knowing that at last the end was in sight.

Internally, however, there was still a lot of work to be done, as the external parameters of my new identity began to take shape. I was more comfortable these days in being identified as a widow, something that had become easier with time. The facts of my widowhood had been staring me in the face for too long, and there was no way in which I could hide. I began to see that I was not alone in my position either, even though I was thirty or forty years younger than most of the other widows I knew. I recognized that there was much I could learn from those who had been bereaved at an older age, and I tried to spend time with some of them as they showered me with love and care, but I felt that

I did not really fit in, as my situation was so totally different from theirs.

Through various avenues I had become aware of an organization called Widowed And Young (WAY), and now it felt right to join. It was a group that had been set up purposely to help people in my situation, and the newsletters helped me to realize that I was not completely alone. The stories they included helped me see that my turbulent emotions were a normal part of the cycle of my grief, and it was comforting to know that there were others who were traversing this rough terrain.

I also came across 'A Different Journey', a forum run by Care for the Family for young widows and widowers, and again subscribed. It felt good to know that there were other Christians who were managing to get through the awfulness of their loss and still retain their hope in God. Their mailings likewise encouraged me to keep going, even though at times it seemed that my pain was pulling me back, and I felt more optimistic as I found that my journey was not as lonesome as I had feared.

But coming to terms with the tag 'widow' was not the only internal battle I had to fight over names; I also needed to learn to accept the title 'single parent'. As I looked back I could see how I had shied away from that label so many times. I cringed as I realized how often I had felt the need to explain the circumstances surrounding my singleness to anyone who would listen, as if by doing so I could set myself apart from those who had been rendered single by other means. The suddenness of Richard's death had thrown me into my grieving unprepared, but it seemed as if there had been some advantages to me. I was so conscious that I had suffered a clean break; I had not endured hideous rejection or abandonment as my long-term partner had walked away, nor had I faced the turmoil of a marriage that had been on the rocks for some time. And yet I found myself being irrationally envious of their position as I imagined the adult dialogues they could still enjoy, and the opportunity to share the parenting load.

However, I also recognized that those who had been through the devastation of a relationship breakdown had been dealt a much more severe blow than I could ever hope to understand. I felt very grateful that there had been no unresolved issues between us when Richard had died, something that had allowed me to move on through my grief with minimal resentment or blame, and, strange though it might sound, I was glad that there had been no protracted or difficult goodbye.

As I reflected on these things, I became aware of how prejudiced and judgmental I had become inside against those who parented alone. I had led such a sheltered life, and knew nothing of their pain. How could I therefore sit in judgment and condemn? To do so was to act in utmost arrogance and attempt to assume the position of God.

All I could do was bow my head in shame and bring my hard heart to God for him to mend once again. In his eyes we were all equal. None of us was better than another, and none of us was worse. He loved us just as we were, whether a single parent or a parent in a husband-and-wife team. And he was the one who wanted to be our provider and our source. For me, the journey to that acceptance had come through the painful valley of my grief. For others God would use a different route, taking the broken pieces of their lives and making something beautiful out of them for him. My job was simply to stand as his child and stay in my story, rather than sit in judgment on anyone else. And so I learned to take on the title of single parent more willingly, without the constant need to explain my circumstances away. Only then was I able to join another organization, Gingerbread, set up to support those who parent on their own.

Lastly, there was the issue of being single as an individual in my own right. It had taken me a long time to stop acting as if I were still one half of a couple, almost having to check myself when I found myself wanting to defer to Richard for his opinion on things. The fact of my widowhood felt like a disability that had been thrust uninvited upon me, and I resented the way it left me feeling so vulnerable and exposed. I found it easier to live in the mentality of feeling my lack, allowing it to remind me of all the things I could not do, rather than looking for the good that was still possible, even though I was on my own. And I compared myself unfavourably to those who continued to parent with their spouse, while looking for people who would rescue me from the pain that this provoked.

Learning to settle into my new status and see the opportunities for learning seemed to take a very long time. I felt swamped by the magnitude of my emotions as I grappled to work out who was left under the tattered ruins of my life, and it took me a long time to recognize that as I suffered, God was suffering too. There were tears in his eyes as I wept, and he felt my pain with a sharpness that even I could not feel. He was not simply holding me up to prevent me from falling into an abyss; he was calling me forth even in the midst of my anguish to find out where my identity really lay. As he steadied my wobbly knees and soothed my frayed nerves, he was bandaging my soul and helping me to find a secure footing in him. He alone was the solid ground underneath the ruins of my life, and he was trying to speak to me through all my heartache and pain.

I found myself returning to the book of Psalms once again, starting with a favourite scripture, Psalm 139, a song written by King David to express something of his wonder at being intimately known and loved by God. It reminded me that God knew all my agony and sorrow, and he had known it from the very start. He had known all the days of my life before I had even experienced one of them. He had known what I would need before I even uttered one sound, and he had slowly been preparing me for this very time. He had walked with me right from the moment of my birth, and even before when I was hidden in the depths of my mother's womb, and he had carried me through. He had seen the joy all over my face as I had learned to intertwine my life around Richard's, and he had wiped the tears from my eyes when I had been distraught with grief as Richard's life had been torn from mine. I could know for certain that God understood my pain.

I read through the other psalms too, coming across ones that I had never noticed before, such as Psalms 13, 28 and 130, songs that cried out to God from the darkness and desolation of an agony too deep for words. My journey through the shadows of death meant I could identify more fully now with their cries of lament, and I knew from experience that God would meet me there.

As I continued to read, I came across a book called *Deeper* by Debbie Alsdorf. It broke through my defences and revealed God's heart towards me in a fresh way. Through its pages I began to hear what God had been trying to tell me for years. I was his. Everything else was superficial and could change. He alone was the constant in my life, and I could trust him.

He wanted me to know that my true identity lay in him and him alone. He knew me far more intimately than I knew myself, and he loved me without reserve. Now he longed for me to know in a deeper way that I belonged to him. How sweet that sounded to my ears. My identity lay purely and simply in him. It wasn't a human type of belonging that would evaporate in time, as my marriage to Richard had done on that fateful night all those months ago. My identity in God as his beloved child was as solid as eternity. I finally knew without a doubt that I belonged. I allowed myself to soak up that truth. I was his. This was the gift that he had been waiting for me to discover through the long days of my grief, the glorious truth that I needed to find for myself.

9 Setting new priorities

The roller-coaster ride of buying a new house was nearly over. The last few weeks had been so full of activity that I had scarcely had a chance to catch my breath. I felt as if my emotional capacity were being stretched to the limit as I said goodbye to the old house and prepared to move to the new. But rather than facing the swirling, heaving mass that lay under the surface, I chose to battle on and keep working through the jobs that had to be done, frustrated that my moods were unstable and it did not take much to send me into a flat spin. Friends were preparing to leave for the other side of the world, and I could barely allow myself to acknowledge their departure for fear that the pain would overwhelm me.

Focusing on anything other than the move felt totally out of the question, and I found myself wishing the time away as I lurched from one day to the next. My moods seemed to swing suddenly and violently from the greatest highs I had experienced for a long time to the most profound lows. I was looking forward with eager anticipation to the chance of making a fresh start, and the opportunity to leave the painful memories of the old house behind, but I was also aware of a deep and searing sense of loss as I bade my farewells to a place that linked me so clearly to Richard and the past.

I found it hard to enjoy the little time we had left as the walls were stripped of their pictures and the remaining household items were packed away. The house felt so desolate and forlorn. My heart wept as I thought back to the empty shell it had been when we had first moved in, an emptiness then that had held such promise and hope. How sad and worn the house looked by comparison now. Where once there had been laughter, fun and games, detailed plans to make things workable and a sense of excitement as new furniture arrived, now there was a feeling of coldness and despair. It was a house I had often struggled to appreciate and enjoy, even when Richard was alive, but now I knew I could not force myself to love it any more. My heart had long since left, and it felt more like a temporary shell that housed us rather than a real home.

After a couple of false starts, the house purchase was finally complete. A great sense of excitement swept over me as I practically skipped down the High Street to collect the keys from the estate agent. It seemed incredible that so many months of tortuous waiting had now come to an end. The house was mine. It felt so unreal, almost too overwhelming for words. My heart sang out to God in praise of all he had done to bring me to this place, and I could hardly keep the smile off my face. I walked around the rooms, deliriously happy for the first time in years. I had made it through the second year of my grief and I was moving on. I knew there would be many more days of pain and sorrow to follow as I continued to break my ties with the past, and I knew that the next few days would be tough in more ways than one, but for now it was enough that God had kept his promise of provision towards me. Even the fact that I was now solely responsible for the upkeep of this property, and the many decisions that would require, did little to dampen my joy. The bit was between my teeth and I was eager to press on. All the planning I had done in the weeks before had finally come to fruition.

Impatiently I set myself the target of a week to prepare the house before we moved in. But before I could even think about doing anything to make it mine, I wanted and needed to give the space to God. Friends offered to come over to pray on that first afternoon, and gladly I accepted. Together we moved around each room, thanking God for the opportunities that each area provided, and asking for his protection from harm and his blessings on its use. It was a lovely way to begin. The children played happily downstairs in the light and airy lounge. My dreams were coming true at last, and it was already starting to feel like our home.

And so began a frenetic week of decorating and cleaning. Paint was slapped on to walls in a flurry of activity that left no room untouched, and I revelled in the feeling of lightness and joy that seemed to permeate the whole house. My daughter's room became a delicate shade of pink, a choice I had been able to give her, and something that Richard might never have allowed. I indulged in colours for the wet areas, and painted the other bedrooms subtle shades of white. And I lightened up the lounge, replacing the rather bright yellow with a warm shade of pale cream. I was delighted that it was all beginning to take shape. Being able to remain at the old house with the furniture and boxes while we accomplished all this made it so much easier than doing it after we moved in.

Each morning we would set out to the new house with painting gear in tow, often taking supplies to last us many hours. Good friends stayed with us for a few days, and their constant enthusiasm kept me going when my energies began to flag. Others nearby offered their services without reservation, often drafting in family members to lend a hand. Friends from the old church as well as the new sacrificially gave of their time and energies to help the endeavour on its way, and I received more help than I knew I would ever be able to repay. It was hard to put into words just how much I appreciated the support, and I felt quite overawed by it all.

The children too helped an incredible amount, wielding paintbrushes whenever they were allowed, and even using their hands at times to cover their bedroom walls with paint. They had endless fun making dens out of the dust sheets, and finding icebergs to bash as the fridge freezer was thoroughly defrosted. They seemed to cope remarkably well with the whirlwind I was inflicting on them, and were thoroughly caught up in the excitement. Each day brought new jobs to attempt along with a different set of friends, and the children seemed to relish working alongside others while I tried to coordinate everything. I felt guilty that I was not giving them much quality time right now, seizing the opportunity to squeeze in extra tasks while help was on hand, and often I relied on others to be more sympathetic to their plight.

As the week gradually disappeared, more friends volunteered to put up shelves and assemble the new pieces of furniture that had arrived in flat-pack form, struggling for hours with awkward shapes in a limited amount of space. I plucked up the courage to ask those with particular skills to lend a hand. The quantity of help I received served to swell my praise to God. I could only trust that God would bless them in their turn.

The decorating done, my attention turned to the boxes that were filling the vicarage study. I felt excited that I could now begin to bring them across to the new house, along with the smaller items of furniture. Friends assisted as I filled up the car with load upon load and ferried them across town. Backwards and forwards we went, almost burning a groove in the roads, while the children had fun riding in the different cars. Many others joined in, some of whom I barely knew, prepared to use their strength and their vehicles to help. I found it hard to take in that all these people loved and cared for me enough to want to assist. It was as if God were determined to show his lavish love for me in practical form. Once more I had to be content to receive, knowing that all he asked of me in return was a grateful heart that acknowledged him.

As the last big push arrived, I knew that the pain was mounting inside. I did not want to stop to think about saying my final goodbyes to the house that had been our home for over three years. My mind drifted back to the last house move we had made, when we had first come to this town. Then we had been travelling across the country with the help of a professional removal firm, and knew barely anyone in the locality. Then I had been heavily pregnant with our son, and our daughter was not yet two years old. Doing it all in one day, with the expectation that Richard would start his job almost immediately, had been a complete headache, and I was glad I was not in that position again. But making this move without Richard was more painful than I wished to acknowledge.

Leaving the old house meant losing a vital link to Richard, one that could never be regained, and it hurt that the new home was one I would never be able to share with him. How I wished that I had at least been able to show him round and share my excitement as the purchase was made. And how I longed for his affirmation that I had made a good choice, and for his practical help and advice. Saying farewell to the vicarage, a place where so many memories had been forged, seemed so odd without him. Even the painful memories of Richard gasping and dying in our bedroom were hard to leave behind.

As the furniture made its way across to the new house, those memories were being torn apart, and although I knew they were forever etched on my heart and mind, it was too painful to think that the physical reminders were being removed. I busied myself as best I could, as if to anaesthetize myself from the pain, and tried to concentrate on the positives that I could enjoy.

Yes, things were different this time around, and we were still three, albeit a different three than when we had first arrived in town. This time I had already made the transition to a new church where I felt at home, and I was surrounded by an army of caring friends, with no impersonal removal firm in sight. How different it all was, and yet how wholesome. Once again I was able to feel deep gratitude towards the one who had brought me thus far and made it all possible.

As we came to the final night in the old house, I valiantly tried to blank out the pain. Now there were no boxes to distract my thoughts, only the bare walls we had decorated and the carpets we had chosen together. The empty shell felt like a loveless tomb. I was embarrassed at how shabby it appeared after months of very little care, and felt ashamed at the amount of cleaning that would need to be done.

Again, friends stepped in and did what I felt unable to do, managing to lavish their love on the vicarage one last time. I could hardly bear to watch. It felt so soulless now, and the bare interior seemed to mock my pain, as if to slice my already battered heart in two. I busied myself at the new house with the children, leaving friends to lock up behind themselves as they finished off at the vicarage. Other friends brought over a meal they had prepared, enough to feed the small army that was in tow, and so gratefully we sat down to eat, yet another amazing example of God's wonderful care.

It was late evening when the final pieces arrived, and the children were already in bed. I was utterly spent and struggling to stay in control. The friends who had been staying had now gone, and it was just the three of us, settling down for the first night in our new home. I knew that I would have to go back to the old house and finish off, but for now all I needed was to sleep. Wearily I headed upstairs, knowing that I still needed to sort out my room. As my head hit the pillow, my thoughts began to whirr. So much had been achieved.

It took me a few days before I felt ready to venture back to the old house and say my final goodbyes. I tried to wander around the rooms as slowly as I dared while the children raced around for one last time. I was filled with gratitude for those who had cleaned up the mess I had left behind. Their work had taken some of the sting away, but even so I wanted to get out. There was no reason for me to be there any more.

In all the headlong rush of the last few weeks, I had forgotten to ask the diocese what to do with the keys, but I knew I did not want them to remain with me. I did not want to be responsible for this place any more. And so I went around to the office at the old church and asked if I could leave the keys there, not sure what else to do. How strange it felt then simply to walk away. Now my ties with the old church were well and truly broken. The pain threatened to overtake me as I drove away, making it hard to enjoy the sense of relief that the saga of moving house was over at last.

The flurry of activity and people had now largely died away, and I began to feel incredibly alone. But the task of unpacking everything and making the house a home was not something I could delegate. I was frustrated that I could not do more, but I knew that the children needed time with me when I was not just focusing on practical tasks. The long school holiday would soon come to an end and then we would have much less time to enjoy being a family. Reluctantly I peeled myself away from the house, trying to invent outings for the children that could be combined with the jobs that needed to be done. Walking into town became a regular activity we could all delight in after months of commuting by car, and so we spent many hours at the playgrounds and other amenities nearby.

As the new term began, I knew there would be yet more changes in our routine, with increasing playgroup sessions for my son. Then my time alone would not be as limited as before. In addition to continuing to help at the church toddler group, I had therefore agreed to take on the relatively onerous task of chairing the playgroup committee, knowing that I needed something to help to fill my time and give me a feeling of purpose outside the home. I was enjoying feeling stronger in myself and having more inner resources, and yet I was also aware that I was still quite fragile and broken within. Living in the new house had left me feeling lighter and freer inside, but the pain of my grief had not completely gone.

A fresh source of anxiety seemed to grip me deep inside. It would not be long until my younger child went to school. I did not know how I would manage to keep myself occupied when I had the whole day alone, and I knew I needed to be proactive in looking for something further to do. The opportunity arose to help in school one morning a week, an idea I had been toying with for some time. But quickly I recognized that I did not have the patience required, and I soon felt unfulfilled. In contrast I was relishing the role of chairperson of the playgroup committee, and the new challenges it was presenting. But I was also aware that my commitment to playgroup would only last until my son went to school. For now, though, it provided the safe environment I needed to test out my resilience while being surrounded by friends. It seemed that it was helping me to rebuild and redefine myself, just as moving house had done.

It was funny to think that Richard might not recognize some aspects of my character now, and I often wondered what I would say to him if he suddenly reappeared. The circumstances of my life had continued to shape me even beyond who I was shortly after Richard had died. I liked to think that he would be proud that I had managed to get through thus far on my own, and knew that he would be overjoyed that my relationship with God was much stronger as a result of the grief I had been through. I was becoming more able to see God's hand at work in the details of my life and to thank him even when things didn't work out. But I also knew that I had a long way to go on the journey of becoming myself.

The task before me now was to work out what was important to me as an individual as I sought to move on. It seemed that many of my values had not changed over time, as I had painfully sought to untangle myself from the identity I had shared with Richard. My walk with God had always been a priority for me, even from an early age, and I knew that that could never change. God had brought me so far on this journey of grief, and had proved his love for me in his faithfulness through all my pain. How could I now turn my back on him, who would never turn from me? In the past my love for Richard had threatened to subsume that love for God, but the long road of grief had shown me so clearly that I could never allow that to happen again. I wanted God always now to be number one.

Second on the list, however, had changed over time. My desire to nurture the children had gradually taken over the place of number two even while Richard had been alive, something that had caused me much pain as I recognized the damage it had done to my marital relationship. But now that Richard was no longer around, the issue was resolved, and I could happily choose to put the children in the exalted place behind my desire to love and serve God.

After that my priorities were a bit trickier to work out. My desire for honesty and integrity in all things had to come in there somewhere, as I abhorred falsity with a passion. That had been part of the battle for me as I had grown through my grief; I knew that I was destroying myself when I chose to act in a way that adopted falsehoods as a cover for my pain, and I felt the inner conflict as I neglected to act from a place of integrity within. It seemed that my longing for authenticity in all I did was a central part of being me.

However, along with these values that I seemed to be bringing from my past, my grief had also unearthed new avenues for me to explore, areas of interest that had lain buried while I had desperately clung on to my roles. My passion for growth was becoming more and more evident, and I knew that I needed to express it in a larger way. Concentrating on my own growth and that of the children was no longer enough. I was looking to expand my horizons in a new and stimulating way.

Again I began reading avidly, this time looking for books that would give me a clue about the future direction I should take. Good friends lent me books and worksheets to help me explore life in a broader way, and I worked through numerous charts, questionnaires and exercises, trying to ascertain my particular strengths and interests. I looked again at the experiences and skills I had already acquired through my former work as a doctor, and sought to identify what was transferable from this field. I dipped into the world of careers guidance, unsure what one did as a doctor if medicine was not the right path. And I spoke at length to anyone who would listen about my quest for a new career goal.

Again my patience was stretched as I tried to run ahead of myself. I wanted to be at the end of the process before I had even begun, and I found it hard to accept that I would have to take time to work through my questions one by one. Equally hard was the ongoing lesson in trust, learning to allow God to take the lead and provide the answers I required, in his time and his way.

There was one certainty that undergirded all my attempts to look wider than the narrow remit I had been trained to operate in. I knew that any work I now did would have to fit around caring for the children. I did not want to parcel them off to after-school care simply so that I could pursue a new career. To do that would be death to myself. Nurturing them was so important to me that if a job required that, I knew I would have to say no. It wasn't simply that I couldn't bear to be parted from them after all we had been through together. It was more a question of the value I placed on being there for them, and the joy and fulfilment that brought.

I knew too that any work I did would have to be stimulating and fun, rather than draining and dull. If not, my life would soon spin out of control as my energy was slowly leeched away. I could not afford for this to happen; life felt precariously balanced as it was, and if I added a demoralizing job into the equation, no amount of money would make it worthwhile. Maintaining the quality of my life as it was, with time and energy enough to do things for myself and the children, rather than having more money to spend on things, was essential to me, and that helped to narrow down the choice.

I could see that resuming my career as a doctor would simply not fit with what I was discovering about myself. For some time I had felt frustrated at how little I could do within that role, feeling that I was metaphorically just sticking plasters on patients' problems, rather than having the time or resources to probe gently deeper inside. It was a highly pressured job with huge time restrictions, and I knew it would crush me if I attempted to return. With a vast amount of courage I finally admitted to myself that my heart was no longer in medicine and I would have to cut my ties. My grief had given me the opportunity to move on in my life; to go back to being a GP would be a backward move for me. I needed a job that would be more creative and less stifling. But as yet I felt unable to relinquish my medical registration, as I was unsure of my future direction. And so the search went on.

One of the many excellent books on grief that I had read in those early days of pain was entitled *Inside Grief* by Kathy O'Brien. It had been both practical and pragmatic, with tips on negotiating a way through the loss involved with widowhood, and anecdotes from Kathy's own journey through pain. I had warmed to her style immediately, and decided to reread the book as I searched for a direction to pursue. At the end was a brief statement: 'Kathy O'Brien is now a life coach.' That intrigued me. What was a life coach? I began to explore.

As I looked at this new possibility, I realized that life coaching encapsulated the essence of what I was looking for in a job: the opportunity to help people grow. It was flexible and individual in the way it was expressed. It would be fulfilling and stretching, and it seemed to offer the mental stimulation I craved. It would also give me an opportunity to use the communication skills I had learnt as a GP, and to practise the parts of medicine I had loved so much, those centred on seeing people as a whole, rather than just a bunch of isolated problems to be fixed. And it seemed to build on the limited amounts of mentoring I had done and enjoyed.

It seemed that life coaching would dovetail with all the experiences I had been through so far, and draw them forward into one coherent whole. Knowing it was an avenue that Richard would have fully endorsed gave me the encouragement to pursue it further. Resigning my medical registration seemed more possible now, and I knew that, if I was to act with integrity, it was something I needed to do. As I sent off the various letters, I felt a huge surge of relief flood my body. Yet another shackle to the past had been broken, and I was free to progress.

After a short search, I found a way of studying that would fit with my requirement for minimal disruption for the children, and I enrolled. The training would take the shape of an intensive weekend course followed by distance learning. I was eager to engage with the material and exercise my brain, and so I threw myself into the pre-course reading as soon as I could. It seemed a long delay until the summer when the weekend training would take place, but this time I was content to wait, enjoying the relative space and freedom.

It was so energizing and liberating to be doing something that fitted so perfectly with my skills and passions, particularly the desire to help others grow.

As I immersed myself in this new venture, I was encouraged to explore more deeply what my priorities in life had become. I knew that I had often craved space, something that I had presumed started as a reaction to the intensity of having pre-school children. But I realized now that the pattern had been in place a long time before. As a wife I had neglected my own need for space, thinking I was being selfish for wanting to be apart from Richard and explore things on my own. I had confused being a good wife with allowing myself to get submerged and subsumed into a joint personality. I had trampled on my need for space in a desperate attempt to bring unity to the whole. How foolish I had been, and how much more fulfilled I would have been as a wife and mother if I had attended to my needs.

I had already identified integrity and authenticity as being vital to me, integral to who I was, and things I couldn't imagine life without. As I dug deeper, I realized that there were other areas I had been sorely neglecting over the years, things that made me feel alive and fulfilled. I struggled to put them into words as they seemed so intangible, and the nearest I could come up with was my enjoyment of exploration, and delighting in childlike fun. My mentor helped me to untangle the various threads and elicit what each value meant to me as the list took shape, and then gently pointed out the ones that I seemed to omit.

I was appalled that God had not been mentioned, as my relationship with him was so central to who I was. I knew that my relationship with him informed everything else I did, but, in my anxiety to find the right words to express myself and make a coherent list, I had forgotten to acknowledge him directly at all! I was grateful that my mentor had been able to spot this obvious omission and carefully reflect it back. Perhaps there was something in there for me to learn too, about directly acknowledging his presence in my life rather than simply assuming he was there.

I came out with a list of eight core values, and, by playing them off one against another, was able to put them in a hierarchy from the most to the least important. It was interesting seeing which of my core values gave way when put to the test. And it was fascinating reflecting on those values and recognizing which ones I was constantly trying to neglect. When I trampled on the things that were so important to me, it left me feeling cheated and unfulfilled. And when I honoured the priorities God had laid deep within, I could see that I would once again be enabled to lead a life that felt rich and full.

10 The baggage of beliefs

It was now over three years since Richard had died. I had survived yet another set of anniversaries without him, and I was feeling much stronger. The training I was undertaking to become a qualified life coach was stimulating and fun, and the exercises I was doing to prepare for work were providing the impetus I needed to keep me moving through my grief. The challenge of reordering my priorities had renewed my hope that life could become fulfilling once again, and I was feeling increasingly positive about what the future would hold.

And yet even as I began to explore the more hospitable landscape of my life, one that was less arid and less dominated by pain, I was aware of a gnawing ache that grumbled on like an undercurrent, affecting everything I did. Despite the lessons I had already learnt and my intense desire to embrace the new, I realized that my grief had not finished with me yet.

The intensive weekend of life-coach training I had undergone had unearthed some pretty ugly stuff inside, stuff that had lain buried and conveniently forgotten for years. Now that the rawness of my grief had eased and my stamina had returned, it seemed that I was being prompted to look deeper within at the unresolved issues and pain I had accumulated.

The emotions I had left untangled there were ones that now filled me with shame. It seemed as if my heart were full of negativity and anger towards so many things, including myself. The thoughts of self-loathing were intense as I acknowledged how much resentment and frustration I had bottled up inside, feelings that I had tried to justify by blaming others and the circumstances in which I had found myself. The impoverished self-esteem that I had attempted to hide behind the cover of my grief was being forced out into the light even as I tried to move on, and I was suddenly being confronted once again by the pervasive sense of inadequacy that had plagued me for many years.

I found myself reliving scenes from the past as if I were rewinding an internal recording, starting at the point of Richard's dying, and going backwards phase by phase.

Slowly I began to acknowledge to myself that the months just prior to Richard's death had been marked by a feeling of intense heaviness and pain. I had felt full of resentment as I had watched Richard's job leech him of his energy and zest for life, and I had felt angry at the demands that had been placed on him. My response to his exhaustion had been to internalize my negative feelings and to struggle on, taking the brunt of the childcare and the running of the house upon myself, while leaving the festering anger inside to turn into feelings of depression and despair. I told myself that I had no right to feel this way, thus destroying what little self-worth remained, and my belief that Richard's job was far more important than anything that I would ever do had only added to my pain.

I recognized that, even in my working environment as a GP, I had battled with a sense of inadequacy and low self-esteem. I had condemned myself as useless when my lack of experience meant I had to ask senior colleagues for help, and

I had felt utterly incompetent when treatment plans that I devised did not work out and my surgeries overran.

But I realized too that the pernicious roots of my feelings of insufficiency came from much further back, something that the vivid flashbacks I was experiencing did their utmost to expose. Memories from the previous parish in which we had lived and worked came rolling through my mind, as I remembered how I had felt overshadowed and insignificant in the light of Richard's job. And I recalled with pain the inadequacy I had felt as I had struggled to embrace mother-hood with ease and grace.

As I looked back over my time with Richard, I could see that there had been many times when my negativity had sought to squash his exuberance and ideas. I had failed to accept the invitation that God had been offering me to view events in a life-giving way, and to exchange my old and wearisome habits of negativity for a way of life that oozed with his joy and love. The damage this had caused was now very evident to me. I had to accept that my negativity had caused much sorrow to Richard and to God, as I had progres-sively allowed it to erode my relationship with them both, as well as doing untold damage to myself.

The negative beliefs had taken a devastating toll on my life and, as I looked back with God's help, I wondered how much they were to blame for the mess I was in now. I had believed for years that I did not deserve to be happily married, and now I was living the reality of that belief. I had thought that life was too tough dealing with the demands of Richard's job alongside the needs of the children, and now that juggling had gone. I had believed that I was inadequate as a clergy wife, and that role had been wrenched from me. I had believed that it was a sign of weakness to admit to needing help, and now, not surprisingly, I found myself alone. And I believed I was incompetent as a mother, something that was making me cling to my children in an unhealthy way.

Over the years since Richard had died, I had done my best to cover my negativity with a thin veneer of pride. I had dealt with many challenges as I had groped my way through grief, and I had managed to draw closer to God along the way. The sad thing was that it seemed as if my low self-esteem hadn't changed much. I still hated the parts of me that didn't conform to my nice little image of what a good Christian should be like. And I was still struggling to accept that I had value in and of myself. I continued to feel that I was not good enough or capable enough to get through life without struggling, and that my opinions were invalid. It was true that I had begun to take hold of God's love for me in a new and much deeper way, and that I could now accept that I was his. And through my journey into grief I had got to the point where I could begin to trust him more. However, the old beliefs remained strangely unmoved in the light of all that I had learnt, and it felt as if they were threatening to lampoon any further efforts I made to move on. It was as if God were peeling back the layers of my resistance to him.

As the flashbacks continued to roll, it seemed as if God were using them to show me how many more negative beliefs I had picked up as I had travelled on, even since my journey into grief had begun: negative beliefs about being inadequate to cope with the future on my own and not being strong enough to make it through my grief intact; pessimistic thoughts about how my circumstances had invalidated my claim to a fulfilling life; destructive beliefs that I was less important than the children and therefore not worth bothering about; vicious beliefs that the only valid contribution I could make to the lives of the children was to meet their physical needs; disabling beliefs that my inability to survive in the workplace as a doctor had disqualified me from ever having a productive working life; and depressing beliefs that my inadequacy as a wife and the fact of my widowhood had ruled out any possibility of my finding love and joy again.

But perhaps the most crucial of all was my belief that I was irretrievably stuck. This was the belief I was using to excuse myself from making any attempt to change because I could reason that it was not my fault. How ridiculous it sounded now that it had been exposed. The belief that had held me captive for so long was no more than an arrogant lie. With God's help it was possible to change how I felt about my life and it was possible to move on. Nothing had been further from the truth when I had believed that I was trapped for ever in my negative approach. I was only as stuck in my pessimism as I had allowed myself to feel, and with God's enabling, I could break free.

Now I could see that my beliefs had caused me to act in the very way that would give them credence to continue. Whenever I had listened to the negative thoughts, I had simply been acting to strengthen their power over me. Now I began to listen in to the internal chatter of my thoughts, utterly appalled at what I heard. My thoughts were full of adjectives that pulled me down, words that described me as too slow, too ugly, too different and too unworthy, words that ran me down and made me feel low about myself in all areas of my life. Listening to that lot every day, it was a wonder that I ever felt positive at all!

Something had to shift if I was to move on into the future intact: my negativity had to go. I did not want to continue on a downward path where I was being swamped by an incessant flow of toxic thoughts, a course of action that was slowly bringing death to my inner parts. I implored God to show me a way through, and as I did so, the coaching exercises I was completing for myself began to take on a whole new meaning and depth.

God was offering me a chance to begin again, setting in place good building blocks for future growth. It was an opportunity to reorder my beliefs in a way that was more honouring to him, and in a way that would allow him to bring life, not death, to my soul. He wasn't the one who was saying I was invalid, inadequate or unlovely. He wasn't condemning me to an unfulfilling life for ever more. He wasn't shouting at me that I was useless as a mother, and that I could not provide adequately for my children's non-physical needs. He wasn't throwing up his hands in horror every time I made a mistake, using it as an excuse to throw me out of his family and deprive me of his love. And he wasn't expecting me to cope with the future on my own without him and to change without his help.

All those negative thoughts were lies, contrary to the truth that he wanted to speak into my life, truth that he knew could set me free, if only I would let it. My negativity had been slowly destroying my relationship with God, with myself and with those around me, and had been utterly dishonouring to him. His ways were so much higher than I had ever dared to imagine, and what he wanted was for me to experience the fullness of joy and the abundance of living that came from trusting in him. He wanted to reclaim the territories of my life that I had given over to fear and the areas that had been full of pain, and suffuse them with his love, in order that I might be free.

The words Richard had quoted so often from John's Gospel came to me again, words that Jesus himself had spoken as he sought to reveal his loving purposes towards those who followed him: 'I have come that they may have life, and have it to the full' (John 10:10). I was not disqualified from this promise by virtue of the grief I was still going through; it was a promise that stood for all people at all times. I felt sad that I had been so slow to grasp this elementary truth that God had been whispering to me through all the years I had walked with him. He did not want me to remain in the shadowlands of fear and anxiety for the rest of my days, nor did he want me to live out only half an existence, hampered by my negativity and despair. He wanted me to come out from behind the flimsy covering of shame I had draped about myself, and to be enveloped by the warm embrace of his truth by accepting that his promise was for me.

I felt as if I were being faced with a profound and fundamental choice. I could either choose to continue to feed myself negative thoughts and beliefs, or I could embrace a new way of being. The choice did not seem all that hard. I had seen all too clearly the effects of my negative beliefs. Instead, I knew I wanted to do life on his terms and in his way, and that meant change.

An old adage that I had first learnt as a trainee health professional came back to me: 'health beliefs govern health actions', a slogan that had been accompanied by a neat little diagram showing how beliefs and actions influenced each other in a cyclical and reciprocating way. Here was something that I could utilize in order to speed things up, and something that my life-coaching training was bringing to the fore. Either I could overhaul my beliefs and my actions would follow suit, or I could change my actions and expect my beliefs to fall into line. I decided to do both simultaneously, just to make sure.

I started by affirming myself with positive comments when I glanced at myself in the mirror, remarking to myself that I looked good or attractive or beautiful, whichever I needed to hear right then. And I began to notice different parts of my body about which I could be positive, reminding myself that it was God's creation, and that he never makes mistakes. I made an effort to dress more carefully, picking colours and clothes that suited me well and felt enjoyable to wear, and I plucked up the courage to have my hair styled in a new way. It felt so radical and so long overdue. The effort soon began to pay off as friends started to comment that I was looking better in myself.

A generous friend paid for me to have a colour-and-style consultation, so I could find out what enhanced my features most, and so I was able to experiment even more. It felt so luxurious and indulgent to play in this way, which in itself did wonders for my posture and my self-esteem. Even more miraculously, I started to enjoy what I saw looking back in the mirror. It felt as if God were the one who was smiling at me from somewhere deep within, as I began to hear his affirmations afresh. I was worthy and valid as a unique individual, and I was allowed to enjoy being me.

That journey begun, I started to address the wider issue of looking after my body. I realized how frequently I had used food to hide behind, seeing it as a ready source of comfort and an acceptable way to medicate my pain. And I noted with horror that what I was pushing into my body in the name of food was merely an indicator of what I thought of myself. When I was feeling unlovely and worthless, I was eating in a way that was not good, and I knew that my greed and overeating did not honour the creation that God had made.

It was my responsibility to look after the body God had given me. I needed to acknowledge to myself that I was worth looking after simply because I was his, and therefore the quantity and quality of the food I ate was a spiritual matter as well as a physical one. What it boiled down to was that eating was an act of worship to him. And so I made changes in my diet, knowing that it was an invitation from God to come closer and experience more of his love.

Exercise was the next area I needed to address. I had already started walking as much as I could, something made infinitely easier by being in the new house. Now I wanted to add a social activity that would complement the style of exercise I had done in the past. Carefully I chose a class that would fit in with my routines. I revelled in the way the movements encouraged me to listen to my body and respect it more and more, and knew that as my body shape changed, my negative beliefs would be on increasingly shaky ground.

Alongside this journey, there was another one on which I needed to embark. It was not enough simply to deal with how I looked after myself; I also had to look at how I related to others as I walked through life. I needed to become aware of who I was being in my day-to-day interactions, and unearth the underlying beliefs that were governing how I responded to others within the roles that I played. It seemed that the place to start that process was in the home, looking again at my role as a mother.

Since Richard's death I had tried to do more and more outside the home, with the result that I had found myself feeling increasingly worn and spent. It was true that I seemed to have more energy these days, and I was enjoying giving out to others more, along with the sense of usefulness and purpose it imbued. But I was aware that the more I took on outside the family, the less I was able to give to the children, leaving them with the dregs of my attention and the meagre scraps of energy that remained. I found myself lashing out at them in impatience when they did not keep up with my frantic pace, and I preferred to focus on meeting their physical needs rather than making myself emotionally available to them. I was trapped in a vicious cycle of my own making as I sought to forge ahead.

I was ashamed that I had let things get to this state, and that the joy had slowly ebbed out of something that had the potential to give me so much delight. My motherhood had become a burden to be endured and an unbearable weight to be lugged around wherever I went, rather than a gift to be treasured and enjoyed.

Slowly it dawned on me that my beliefs were to blame. My feelings of inadequacy in my motherhood were profound, and almost as deep as the sense of inadequacy in myself. As I began to recognize what was going on, I realized how much energy I was using to keep those negative beliefs alive. Surely that energy could be released and used in a more productive way? Instead of dwelling on the unconstructive words I felt described my current level of parenting, I needed to look for adjectives to describe the type of mother I longed to be. I trawled through my mind for words that would encapsulate what being a good mother meant to me.

The children were still young, even though they were now both at school. My time with them was much more limited than it had once been, and so being available when they were around needed to be a priority for me. When I did see them, I wanted to be patient with them, rather than snapping at them whenever I opened my mouth. I asked for God's help as patience had never come easily. Loving them had to come in there too, as a prerequisite to all that I did, and I wanted to incorporate a good smattering of fun. I now regarded it as a compliment when my children told me I was 'too silly', and I loved hearing their laughter when we did funny dances together or played daft pretend games.

What it came down to was that I wanted to be a fun, patient, loving and available mother. Those four adjectives summed up how I wanted to be. I put them into a sentence as a statement of my intent: 'I am willing to be a loving, patient, available and fun mother.' I couldn't yet say that that was what I was, but I stated my willingness to learn.

I wrote the sentence on a piece of coloured paper and stuck it on the kitchen wall to remind myself of my aims, and I chose to renew my commitment to it every day, asking God to help me to become that kind of mum.

When I found myself struggling, as I often still did, I would look at that list on the wall and pick out just one of the qualities to focus upon; doing it that way made it seem more manageable. And as I began to internalize the sentence, I found myself asking how a mother who was patient, loving, available and fun would react in different situations, thus giving me more food for thought. My hope was that over time I would begin to see some impact on my family life, but even if I didn't, I felt calmer in myself just knowing that I was on the right track. I wasn't beating myself up inside any more and I was starting to recover; having a goal in sight meant that I could refine my efforts in a way that would eventually pay off.

Decisions about how I spent my time could now be made by measuring up potential opportunities against my aims and gracefully shelving those that pulled me away. Gradually my time with the children was becoming more enjoyable again, as I poured my energies into becoming the right kind of mum. Mentally I was being transformed as my negative thoughts gave way to more affirming ones, and I was able to relax more into my mothering and learn to be more fully present in it as myself. And as I made that shift I was able to recognize that I had been running away from one of the biggest gifts God had ever sought to bless me with, the role of my motherhood, and mothering my children in my own individual way.

As this learning continued, I felt encouraged to look at different areas of my life. I drafted sentences stating my intentions for the different roles I played, and began to declare who I was willing, with God's help, to become. And to these sentences I added others about being willing to be surrendered and yielded to God, and to be a channel for his love to flow through. These intentions became the backbone of my new belief structure, and together with the reminder that I was his beloved child, they were the tools God was using to help me change and grow.

11 Transitioning grief

The New Year had come around again, and as before I was gripped by an immense feeling of weariness as I sought to move on. The months up to Christmas had seen me pushing myself to the brink of exhaustion in order to complete my life-coaching qualification, and I desperately longed for some space in my schedule. The simultaneous exercise of reordering my beliefs had been gruelling at times, as I had endeavoured to make good endings with the past, and I was grateful that for now at least the vivid flashbacks had come to an end. Keeping in touch with my present reality had been really hard while they had filled my mind.

I felt I had passed through some pretty rocky terrain as God had showed me the squalor that lay in my heart, and not surprisingly it had taken its toll. I longed for a chance to recuperate and rest, and knew I needed to slow down. But slowing down was something that I still struggled to do. The impetus of getting thus far made me restless to continue, and I was desperate not to lose the momentum I had gained.

It seemed as if a great battle were going on within me as I tried to accept the tension between the two poles. Moving forward with integrity while making peace with the past in an ever-deepening way was something I was still struggling to do. I could now thank God for the part that Richard had played in my life without constantly being ambushed by tears. And I could thank him too for the ways he had worked in my life since Richard had gone. Yet my desire to move on to the next thing meant that I often failed to enjoy the present and savour the sense of achievement at how far I had already travelled.

I felt as if I were being pulled in two inside as the past and future met in me, each one clamouring as loudly as they dared to be heard. The work on beliefs and priorities had brought me to the realization that it was okay for me to enjoy life again, and I knew that being in the moment rather than always racing ahead was something I needed to focus on. But I was still too good at driving myself, and so I tried to push ahead to find alternative avenues to explore.

I had found the life-coaching training to be so stimulating and fun that I wondered if I should go on and do some more. My mind was enjoying the challenges of building a new career, and the reading and exercises I had worked through as a result had made a profound impact on my life. I decided to enrol in another long-distance learning scheme, feeling that this was something I could now undertake.

But the lack of joy I soon felt at my swift decision began to erode my still-fragile sense of peace. Reluctantly I had to let it go, feeling foolish that I had tried to rush ahead once again without considering the wider cost to us all. Now was not the time to embark on something as intensive as this when I remained very tender and broken within. I had to accept that I was weak inside from the grief I had been walking through, and that I could not simply push on into the future without due regard for the past, no matter how strong the urge to leave it all behind.

The treacherous path that God had taken me on had caused me much heartache within, as he had shown me how impoverished my view of him had been. It had caused me to search deeper than I ever thought possible, and to look at the scars in my life that were dishonouring to him. And it had felt at times as if my life were a very frail craft on a vast and turbulent sea with little hope of making it to land. But throughout the pain there had been moments of deep joy and hope that a new beginning would one day come, acting as glimpses of light to encourage me to continue moving on. It seemed that my capacity to feel both joy and pain had been slowly enlarged as I had journeyed through my grief, and I often felt that there was a very fine dividing line between the two.

My life now bore barely any resemblance to the life I had once shared intimately with Richard. The stark physical reminders of his absence were no longer surrounding me at every turn, and better days even tried to convince me that my grief work was complete. My new-found sense of identity and purpose was growing ever more secure, and I no longer felt compelled to hide myself behind the children all the time.

And yet acute pangs of loss would still overwhelm me unexpectedly now and then, ambushing my plans and leaving me reeling once again. These pangs felt so incongruous three and a half years down the line, and the shock at their appearance seemed to mock the normality I had sought to rebuild. The wound of my grief, although healing well, was still quite fresh and new, and I had to allow for the fact that I still remained somewhat broken within.

Facing the fact that I would probably always have moments when the ferocity of the pain would strike out of the blue was a bitter pill to swallow. I longed to leave the anguish behind and be free to embrace the new, and felt frustrated that the two should want to co-exist. Accepting that I would always walk with a limp was not what I had in mind.

But as the warmth of the spring made itself felt, it seemed as if the stormy seas were starting to settle and the clouds were beginning to clear at last. The brakes of pain that had caused me to hang back for so long were slowly being removed, and I was being invited to explore the vast new world that opened in front of me, as if I had become a little child once again. I looked about in wonder as I saw evidence of God's goodness all around. Gradually my grip was loosening on the story of my grief, and the scenery was changing yet again.

However, as the familiar contours of my pain began to fade, I found myself floundering and uncertain as to how to go on. The new beginnings seemed so tentative and unsure, as yet uncharted ground, and I had no idea what God might have in store. I felt unnerved by this new territory where the landscape was less fearsome and more lush, and I felt lost without the constant presence of my grief. I had no framework to make sense of this strange new terrain, and as I edged my way along, my emotions became labile once again. I swung from high points of exhilaration when new ideas began to emerge and life seemed to flow with ease, to low points of immense frustration as I grappled with my impatience to leave the past behind. Why was I having so much trouble now that all the major physical changes had been made?

Metaphors and mixed metaphors were as close as I could get to articulating how I felt. Somehow it seemed as if the cocoon of my grief were slowly beginning to open to make way for the new life to emerge, even though it was not yet clear what form that new life would take.

Once again I began to read, this time a book called *Transitions* by William Bridges. Here at last was someone who understood the journey that I was on. The transition I was undergoing was a normal part of the process of change that had been thrust upon me when Richard had died. My inner journey of transition was meant to take much longer than the physical changes, and I could not hurry it along. The psychological aspects of my grief needed a chance to catch up with the external events of my life, and if I tried to speed them up, I would only end up circumventing the process and potentially damaging myself. As the fragile chrysalis of my pain split open with the warmth of the sun, the delicate new wings of the butterfly needed to be allowed to unfold and dry out if they were to be strong enough to fly, and the waiting this entailed was an integral part of the transition.

What I was experiencing was not a figment of my imagination, nor an unhealthy response to my grief. Rather it was a natural process that was common to us all. The endings I had sought to make with the past were a vital first step in my transition through grief, and the long nights of agony as I had tried to wrestle my own self from the joint identity we had once held had been a central part of this journey within. Looking at the times when I had let Richard down by not allowing him fully to express himself, and the ways I had been so much less than the person God had created me to be, had been a crucial part of my passage through grief, as had the process of making peace with myself about the things I could not now change. The emotions that I had poured out on paper to God in my journal had enabled me to work through my feelings of remorse until I was able to let them go, and through them I had learnt that I could surrender my pain to God with open hands, knowing that he alone was the one who could redeem.

The signs of new beginnings had been appearing for some time, advance promises that what was not yet in tangible form would one day arrive. Different vistas were opening up as I surveyed the land around, and although the view seemed shrouded in mist, I could see enough to know that I longed to get closer and go further. It seemed as if the glimmers of hope that had sustained me through the gruelling journey of grief were longing to be fulfilled.

But for now I was in an in-between time, a neutral zone or a void, where the old way of life had all but disappeared and the new was not yet fully present. In this neutral zone I could expect my feelings to be turbulent as I found myself torn between the future and the past. It was reasonable to long for closure and completion as I sought to move ahead and leave my grief behind. And it was okay sometimes to wish that I could return to the good old days of hiding behind the familiarity of my pain, with the safe and comfortable ways of behaving that I had clung to for so long, even though I knew that if I did so for any length of time, it would slowly cause me to die within.

Through the book on transitions, I learnt that I was expected to feel frustrated by the seeming lack of activity as time stretched on with little sign of movement. It seemed as if this waiting time and the frustration it bore were a further opportunity to draw closer to God and trust him that the new things he had in store for me would eventually come. I was meant to be searching the horizon eagerly, yearning for some glimpse of the future. And it was legitimate to feel myself being torn in two inside, even as these opposing feelings sought for supremacy within. There was no shame in feeling lost in this in-between land, and I could allow myself to articulate how I felt, knowing that God understood my confusion and restlessness.

The challenge for me was to enjoy the space of this time of waiting. It was a chance for my creativity to come to the fore, and an opportunity for me to try out new ideas, a time to consolidate what I had already learnt on my journey through grief, and to thank God for all that he had done inside my heart. And it was the opportunity I needed to explore new ways of being, ones that I had been too afraid to embrace before, and ones which I would be able to carry on into the future.

As I looked at this in-between time with fresh eyes, I saw that it had come at exactly the right time. I needed this resting place, and I knew that if I allowed him to, God would use it to further the work he had begun in me. This neutral zone had, in fact, been present for a little while now, running concurrently with the endings as they had been made and the new beginnings as they had emerged. The three stages of the transition had not run in a neatly linear fashion, each waiting patiently for their turn to appear. Rather they had been overlapping processes, each phase informing the others, and each thread important and necessary for the work that was underway.

As I reread the book, I began to appreciate more fully the bigger picture of the journey I was on and find my bearings in this unfamiliar landscape. It was enough that I was not alone and that God had met me on this foreign ground. Although I had no indication when the scenery would change to a more favourable aspect, I felt more settled within. Once more God had brought me to a place where I was learning to trust him and acknowledge that he was in control.

Now a new feeling began to arise within me, one that I had not had for some time. A sense of gratitude began to spring up out of the deep wells of my heart as I looked back and saw the gifts that God had strewn along my way.

These gifts were so much grander than anything I could have conceived. Instead of hand-finished chocolates and beautiful flowers, he had carried me carefully through tempestuous seas, in order that I might realize how faithful was his love towards me. Instead of pretty jewels and witty books, he had showered me with trying circumstances so I might discover him waiting in the depths of my heart. And instead of woollen jumpers and flimsy ornaments, he had lavished me with anguished thoughts and recurrent pain that had made me look ever deeper within.

There had been no pretty wrapping paper or coloured bows to alert me to the fact that these were gifts, and no tags or handwritten cards with lovely sentiments attached, and yet they had all been given freely and without reserve, knowing that these were the very gifts I most needed to receive. These offerings, so often ones that I had mis-construed, had called me ever forward into the knowledge of God's awesome love, and had drawn me to his side. I could only bow my head in wonder at how he had accomplished such a thing, and thank him for the storms he had brought.

My mind was in a whirl as I sought to understand this new-found grace. Acknowledging that God had allowed Richard to die and had used the resulting desolation in my life for good was as near as I could get to expressing the mystery it entailed.

I would never know exactly what had happened to make Richard die that night, or what had gone on in the spiritual realm to bring him to that point. And I would never appreci-ate the far greater picture of his death from God's vantage point, or why God had allowed it. From where I stood, Richard's death had not been negotiable at any point, and he had been promoted while I had been left to carry on.

Nor could I believe that Richard's death had been insti-gated purely to allow me to grow. To do so would be to believe in a much smaller god than the one I had come to know. The God who had revealed himself to me through the long months of my grief was a God who desired to show compas-sion and love to all his creatures in a way that brought life to each one. And yet through all the brokenness and grief, it seemed that God had been at work. I could only marvel at the way that he was able to bring good out of such devast-ation and pain.

But even as I acknowledged my gratitude to God for the way he was working in me, it felt as if he were beckoning me even deeper within, to express a gratitude far beyond anything I had yet known, a gratitude that could come only from him.

As I reviewed where I had come from, I found myself thanking God for the gift of my pain. On a human level it felt shocking beyond belief, and I felt ridiculous and stupid even as I heard the words rise up from deep inside. And yet even as I tried to deny them, they began slowly to unfold their wings. Out of the barrenness of the void I now found myself in, a beautiful butterfly was starting to emerge. I found myself gasping in wonder as I looked at what God was doing in me.

It seemed now as if all the other gifts, complete with their prickles and thorns, had been merely paving the way for this bigger gift to appear. Each one had been a tiny fragment of the whole, and each one had been a vital part of what God was doing under the surface of my life as he had performed his surgery deep within. All these smaller gifts, each precious in their own right, had given me glimpses of the greater gift of his love that God wanted to endow, and through them all I was getting the message loud and clear: God loved me.

Once again I found myself overwhelmed by the magnitude of his amazing love. It was a love that was so secure in who he was and in the knowledge that my identity lay in him that he had been willing to risk it all on a gift, knowing that at any time I could throw it back in his face and turn away from him. This beautiful gift, so barbed and covered with many thorns that had the potential to pierce me with such deep pain, was something he had held out to me for so long, knowing that it was exactly what I needed to allow me to grow. It was a gift that I had refused to accept so many times, preferring the comfort of dwelling in the familiar self-pitying grooves of my pain. And yet he had persistently held it out to me in love. My mind could scarcely take it in: my grief was a priceless and precious gift from him. Such love as this was too much for me to comprehend.

Nothing I had ever done had made me worthy to receive such a costly gift as this, and I could only stand in awe at the one who had made it possible for me to get to this place. He alone was the one who had accompanied me through the dark alleys and tear-stained nights of my anguished soul, and he alone had drawn me on.

This gift of grief was so delicate and fragile. It was a gift that I could never have desired to receive from his hands; to do so would have been to negate my love for Richard, the one whom I had built my life around and who had shared so much of God's love and grace with me. And yet the gratitude within me would not abate, and I found myself thanking God for the fact that Richard had gone. It felt abhorrent that I should even use those words, and I knew that many would not understand. How could I say that I was grateful for the opportunities that his death had provoked without feeling disloyal to Richard's name? How could I admit to others that I would not change what I had been through for the world, when at the same time I still desired to be with him as his wife? It felt too close to mystery here, and I simply could not hope to understand.

Through all the desolation God had been wooing me to himself. How could I then continue to ignore the invitation of his love? It seemed as if he were gently enabling my hands to uncurl so I could take hold of the gift of grief. And as I did so, I realized that he was enabling me to accept that my grief had indeed been a costly gift from him.

It seemed as if God were already beginning to redeem my loss in an unexpected but beautiful way, one I hoped would give much glory back to him.

Appendix: Further sources of support

The WAY Foundation (Widowed And Young)
A volunteer-run charitable organization for those aged fifty or under when their partner died.

Provides a regular newsletter, local groups in many regions, member-organized holidays and short breaks, a helpful book and video loan service, and a secure online message board.

Website: www.wayfoundation.org.uk
Email: info@wayfoundation.org.uk
Address: PO Box 6767, Brackley NN13 6YW
Telephone: 0870 011 3450

Care for the Family
Care for the Family is a UK-wide charity with a Christian ethos, serving those of all faiths and none. A branch called 'A Different Journey' supports those who have lost their partner to death at a young age, through events, a telephone befriending service, email newsletters and web resources.

Website: www.careforthefamily.org.uk
Email: mail@cff.org.uk
Telephone: 029 2081 0800

Gingerbread

A charitable organization designed to assist lone parents and provide information and support.

Provides regular newsletters and a whole range of member benefits, information leaflets, local support groups and a lone parent helpline.

Website: www.gingerbread.org.uk

Email: membership@gingerbread.org.uk or via website

Address: Gingerbread, 255 Kentish Town Road, London
   NW5 2LX

Telephone: 020 7428 5400

Lone Parent Helpline: 0800 018 5026
   (Mon – Fri 9am to 5pm, Wed 9am to 8pm)

The following secular organizations also offer help to the bereaved in different ways.

Cruse Bereavement Care is the largest bereavement support charity in the UK and helps many thousands of people/children each year through one-to-one support, groups, resources etc.

SOBS (Survivors of Bereavement through Suicide) is the only organization specifically helping those bereaved through suicide.

Winston's Wish is the largest UK charity supporting bereaved children (and their families).

Books I have found helpful in my journey through grief:

Debbie Alsdorf, *Deeper: Living in the Reality of God's Love* (Revell, 2008).

William Bridges, *Transitions: Making Sense of Life's Changes* (Da Capo Press, 2004).

Kathy O'Brien, *Inside Grief: Overcoming the Loss of a Loved One* (Authentic Media, 2004).

Jennifer Rees Larcombe, *Beauty from Ashes: Readings for Times of Loss* (Bible Reading Fellowship, 2000).